What's Happening?

Reading Strategies with Informational Text

Lawrence Gable

Dr. Ron Klemp

Dr. Bill McBride

HOLT McDOUGAL

 HOUGHTON MIFFLIN HARCOURT

COVER
Photo Credits
bkgd: Corbis, (l) Comstock/Getty Images, (r) Ryan McVay/PhotoDisc/Getty Images.

ISBN 13: 978-0-547-746050

6 7 8 9 10   0982   20 19 18 17 16 15 14

4500459873   A B C D E F G

What's Happening?
Table of Contents

What's Happening Reading Lessons

Name _____ Date _____

ANTICIPATION GUIDE

Directions: <u>Before</u> you read the article "Questions Linger About Tasers," read the statements below. If you agree with a statement, put a check on the line. Otherwise, leave it blank.

_____ **1.** Police should use any force needed to stop suspects.

_____ **2.** People who commit crimes should not have rights.

_____ **3.** Police don't care about how much force they use.

Once you have checked the statements above, tell why you agreed or disagreed with each statement in the section below.

1. _____

_____

2. _____

_____

3. _____

_____

In the box below, draw a picture of what you think this article is about.

By Lawrence Gable
© 2010 What's Happening Publications

Subject: Human Rights

Questions Linger About Tasers

The Taser has become a weapon of controversy in police departments. Sometimes these electrostun weapons are safe, but they have contributed to some deaths. In addition, nobody really knows if there are other long-term dangers. Several human rights organizations have asked police to stop using Tasers until they know more.

A Taser looks like a gun. Instead of bullets, it shoots a 50,000-volt charge of electricity. The Taser shoots two little hooks at the end of copper wires. They can hit a person 21 feet away. The effect is strongest when the hooks enter the victim's skin. The shock also can pass through two inches of clothing.

The shock is short, but powerful. It causes pain and paralysis for five seconds, and it usually knocks the victim to the ground. In those few seconds officers usually can gain control of the person.

The Taser is not the first weapon to shoot an electric current. The first stun guns shot darts, and later models shot hooks. They were hard to handle, so few police departments used them. The Taser gun is ten times more powerful than the old stun guns.

The Taser's appeal has been its safety. It can reduce injuries to officers and suspects. An officer does not need to use a nightstick or pepper spray, and does not need to struggle with a suspect.

It took a few years to learn how police departments are using Tasers. Reports showed that police use them most often on people who are unarmed. Police have shocked people who are already in handcuffs. They also have shocked children, the elderly, and pregnant women.

Questions continue about the effects of electric current on people. A short, weak current probably will not harm a healthy person. For people with weak hearts, though, a strong shock can cause a heart attack. It also can affect the hearts of people taking medications. Nobody knows yet what the effects are on people who have diseases like Parkinson's or multiple sclerosis. Tasers may harm pregnant women and children too.

Some police officers at schools also carry Tasers. Doctors say that the current is more intense in a small body. The voltage could cause damage in developing nerves, muscles and brains.

It is still not clear when it is appropriate to use a Taser. Some police around the country already have limited their use. After several deaths in Las Vegas, the department stopped using them on people in handcuffs. It also discouraged multiple shocks. Some police chiefs stopped using Tasers until they knew more about their safety.

Amnesty International is one organization that asked police to limit the use of Tasers. It reported that Tasers had been involved in almost 100 deaths. The organization also asked police to stop using it on children and the elderly unless they threaten to harm themselves or others.

Most people agree that Tasers can help police. As with any weapon, there is some risk of physical injury to the victim. When researchers learn more about those risks, police will know better when it is appropriate to use Tasers.

REACTION GUIDE

Directions: <u>Now that you have read</u> "Questions Linger About Tasers," reread the statements below. Then think about how the author would feel about these statements. If you think the author would agree, put a check on the line before the number. Then, below the statement, copy the words, phrases, or sentences in the article that tell you the author's real views.

_____ **1.** Police should use any force needed to stop suspects.

Article notes: _____

_____

_____

_____ **2.** People who commit crimes should not have rights.

Article notes: _____

_____

_____

_____ **3.** Police don't care about how much force they use.

Article notes: _____

_____

_____

WORDSTORM

Directions: It's good to know more than just the dictionary definition of a word. A wordstorm lets you write down information that helps you understand what a word means, how it's related to other words, and how to use it in different ways.

What is the word?

controversy
_____

Copy the sentence from the text in which the word is used:

_____

_____

What are some other words or phrases that mean the same thing?

_____

What are three things people might do during a controversy?

1. _____ 2. _____ 3. _____

Name three people who would likely use this word other than

teachers.

1. _____ 2. _____ 3. _____

Draw a picture that reminds you of the word "controversy" below:

TIME MY READ # 1

Directions: With a partner, you will see how many words you can read correctly in 45 seconds. As you read, your partner will put an "X" through any word read incorrectly. Then your partner will read while you keep score. When you have both read, trade your books or papers. Count the total number of words you read correctly. Write this score at the bottom of your page.

WORD COUNT

long-term organizations electricity current powerful Taser healthy control	8
appeal departments reduce current weapon safety injuries victim	16
paralysis suspects unarmed medications impact research nervous diseases	24
long-term organizations electricity current powerful Taser healthy control	32
appeal departments reduce current weapon safety injuries victim	40
paralysis suspects unarmed medications impact research nervous diseases	48
long-term organizations electricity current powerful Taser healthy control	56
appeal departments reduce current weapon safety injuries victim	64
paralysis suspects unarmed medications impact research nervous diseases	72
long-term organizations electricity current powerful Taser healthy control	80

Number of words read correctly _____.

ECHO READING

Directions: When you read, you should make breaks between groups of words. As the teacher reads each phrase, repeat aloud what was read and underline that phrase. Then you will read the whole sentence aloud together. The first sentence has been underlined for you.

Tasers are becoming a popular weapon in police departments. In some situations these electro-stun weapons are safer than others. They have contributed to some deaths, however, and nobody really knows if there are other long-term dangers. Now several human rights organizations are asking police to stop using them until further research is done.

A Taser looks like a gun. Instead of bullets, it shoots 50,000 volts of electricity. The current comes from batteries, and a nitrogen cartridge supplies power for the shot. When an officer pulls the trigger, the Taser shoots two barbs that are like small fishhooks. They are attached to the end of copper wires, and they can hit a person 21 feet away.

"Questions Linger About Tasers"

GET A CONTEXT CLUE

Directions: Below are sentences from "Questions Linger About Tasers." Read the sentence. Look back in the article and read the paragraph the sentence is in. Circle what you think is the best answer to each question.

"In addition, nobody really knows if the Taser causes *long-term* dangers."

1. The word "long-term" means:

    A. instant
    B. lasting effects
    C. bad
    D. alongside

"The *effect* is strongest when the hooks enter the victim's skin."

2. An "effect" is:

    A. an outcome or result
    B. a collision
    C. a warning
    D. a loud noise

"It can reduce injuries to officers and *suspects*."

3. The word "suspects" means:

    A. police officers
    B. doctors
    C. people thought to be guilty
    D. people who fight criminals

"The Taser's *appeal* has been its safety."

4. The word "appeal" has to do with:

    A. attraction
    B. hazard
    C. a court decision
    D. a lack of decision

"It can also affect the heartbeat of a person taking certain *medications*."

5. The word "medications" means:

    A. exercises
    B. substances used by the police
    C. medicines used with illness
    D. doctors and nurses

"Doctors say the *current* is much more intense in a small body."

6. The word "current" is related to:

    A. electricity
    B. law
    C. warfare
    D. police officers

WORD CHOICE

Directions: As you read this piece, you will find blanks for missing words. Three words are listed after the blank. One of these is correct. <u>Read the rest of the sentence past the blank to figure out which is the correct word</u>. Write it in the blank.

Tasers are becoming a popular weapon in police departments. In some situations these electro-stun _____ (voltage, weapons, safety) are safer than others. They have _____ (excitement, found, contributed) to some deaths, however, and nobody _____ (really, never, wonders) knows if there are other long-term _____ (shock, organizations, dangers). Now several human rights organizations are _____ (asking, want, wish) police to stop using them until _____ (further, often, never) research is done.

A Taser looks _____ (like, some, just) a gun. Instead of bullets, it _____ (holds, fire, shoots) 50,000 volts of electricity. The current _____ (comes, start, will) from batteries, and a nitrogen cartridge _____ (give, supplies, send) power for the shot. When an officer _____ (pull, pulls, pulling) the trigger, the Taser shoots two _____ (barbs, barb, barbed) that are like small fishhooks. They _____ (are, is, be) attached to the end of copper _____ (wires, wired, wiring) and they can hit a person 21 feet away.

Name _____ Date _____

LOOK WHO'S TALKING

Directions: Below are references from "Questions Linger About Tasers." Number each paragraph. Look back in the article and re-read the paragraph in which you find the reference. Circle what you think is the best answer to each question.

1. **In the last sentence of paragraph one, the word "they" refers to:**

   A. Human rights organizations
   B. Tasers
   C. police
   D. effects

2. **In paragraph two, the word "they" refers to:**

   A. the bullets
   B. the charge
   C. the hooks
   D. the victims

3. **In paragraph four, the word "they" refers to:**

   A. the Taser
   B. the first stun guns
   C. the darts
   D. the departments

4. **In paragraph seven, the word "it" refers to:**

   A. the heart
   B. the person
   C. the people
   D. the current

5. **In paragraph nine the word "it" refers to:**

   A. the department
   B. the Taser
   C. the shocks
   D. the time to use the Taser

6. **In paragraph ten, the word "It" refers to:**

   A. Amnesty International
   B. Tasers
   C. The organization
   D. Police department

NOTE MAKING

Directions: Read the key **bold** words on the left side of the chart below. Then add notes that answer the question in parentheses under the key word.

Human Rights Organizations (What?)	
Taser (How?)	
Police (Why?)	
Effects on people (What?)	
Restrictions on use (Where?)	

IS THAT A FACT?

Directions: Read the definitions of a *fact* and an *inference* below. Then read the paragraph that follows. At the bottom of the page, write an "F" on the blank if a sentence is a fact. Write an "I" if the sentence is an inference. Use the following definitions:

Fact – a statement that can be proven to be true from the article.

Inference – a guess as to what MIGHT be true.

Tasers are a popular weapon in police departments. Sometimes these electro-stun weapons are safe, but they have contributed to some deaths. In addition nobody really knows if there are any other long-term dangers. Now several human rights organizations are asking police to stop using Tasers until they know more. The Taser's appeal has been its safety. It can reduce injuries to officers and suspects. An officer no longer needs to use a nightstick or pepper spray, and does not need to struggle with a suspect.

_____ **1.** Police like to use Tasers because they can be more effective with suspects.

_____ **2.** Some human rights organizations are against the use of Tasers by

police officers.

_____ **3.** We don't know enough about how the Taser really works on people.

_____ **4.** The use of the Taser seems to be increasing.

_____ **5.** The use of the Taser can sometimes result in a fatality.

_____ **6.** It is not known how the Taser affects a person over time.

MAKE A SPACE

Directions: Below are sentences that are missing punctuation and capitalization. First, draw slash marks (/) between the words. Then rewrite each sentence in the space below it, filling in the missing punctuation and capitalization.

Example:

tasers/are/becoming/a/popular/weapon/in/police/departments

Tasers are becoming a popular weapon in police departments.

---

1. theshockisshortbutpowerful

_____

2. ithastakenafewyearsforthepolicetolearnhowtousetasers

_____

_____

3. somepoliceofficersatschoolscarrytasers

_____

_____

4. doctorssaythatthecurrentismoreintenseinasmallbody

_____

_____

Name _____ Date _____

TIME MY READ # 2

Directions: With a partner, you will see how many words you can read correctly in 45 seconds. As you read, your partner will put an "X" through any word read incorrectly. Then your partner will read while you keep score. When you have both read, trade your books or papers. Count the total number of words you read correctly. Write this score at the bottom of your page.

long-term organizations electricity current powerful Taser healthy control	8
appeal departments reduce current weapon safety injuries victim	16
paralysis suspects unarmed medications impact research nervous diseases	24
long-term organizations electricity current powerful Taser healthy control	32
appeal departments reduce current weapon safety injuries victim	40
paralysis suspects unarmed medications impact research nervous diseases	48
long-term organizations electricity current powerful Taser healthy control	56
appeal departments reduce current weapon safety injuries victim	64
paralysis suspects unarmed medications impact research nervous diseases	72
long-term organizations electricity current powerful Taser healthy control	80

Number of words read correctly _____. Is the score higher

than it was in Time My Read #1?_____

WORD PARTS

Directions: The Latin root "medicus" means *physician* or *doctor*. Read the definitions below. Then draw a picture of what each word means.

1. **medicine** – (noun) something one takes to treat an illness or injury.

2. **medic** – (noun) a doctor or student learning to be a doctor, often working in a war zone.

3. **medical** – (adjective) having to do with one's health, a hospital, or a doctor; for example, a medical emergency.

4. **medicinal** – (adjective) something that is meant to cure you, or something that has a bad taste .

medicine	medic	medical	medicinal

Directions: The Latin root "poli" means *city*. Each of the following words has the root "poli" in it: politics, metropolitan, police, politician. On each blank, write the word that describes the picture.

_____ _____ _____ _____

TASER WORD PUZZLE

Directions: Complete the crossword puzzle.

Across

2 someone elected to work for government

4 a disagreement about something

6 people thought to be guilty

9 an outcome or result

10 something with a bad taste

Down

1 a city

3 lasting a long period of time

5 an attraction

7 someone who enforces the law

8 a doctor working in a war zone

Word List

METROPOLIS	MEDICINAL	MEDIC	CONTROVERSY	EFFECT
APPEAL	POLICE	POLITICIAN	SUSPECTS	LONG-TERM

WRITING FRAME

Directions: Below is a writing frame. Use your knowledge and information from the article to complete the frame below.

A Taser looks like a gun, and shoots _____

volts _____. The shock comes from two

_____ that look like _____.

The reason why police officers like the Taser is _____

_____. They feel that they can be more effective in

_____ who commit

_____. Reports claim that police use Tasers on

people who are _____. This is why human

rights organizations think that _____.

There have been questions raised about how the Taser affects

the body, and there are cases where _____.

Amnesty International, a human rights organization, is asking

that _____. At least when we learn

more about the Taser, it can be used _____

_____.They feel that the Taser should

not be used until _____

_____.

TAKE A STAND

Directions: People often have different feelings, or opinions, about the same thing. A "debate" is when people argue their different ideas. A good, persuasive argument has the following:

Facts – statements that can be proven to be true.

Statistics – research from a scientific study that uses numbers.

Examples – stories from the world that support an opinion.

You and a partner are going to debate two of your other classmates. The topic you are going to debate is the following:

Police should be able to use any force needed to stop a suspect.

Decide whether you agree or disagree with this statement.
Then answer these questions in order to win your debate.

1. What are your 2 strongest points to persuade the other side?
(You can do Internet research to include facts, statistics, and examples.)

A. _____

B. _____

2. What will the other side say to argue against point A?

_____

3. What will the other side say to argue against point B?

_____
_____

4. What will you say to prove the other side's arguments are wrong?

_____
_____
_____

ASSESSMENT

Comprehension: Answer the questions about the passage below.

Tasers are becoming a popular weapon in police departments. In some situations these electro-stun weapons are safer than others. They have contributed to some deaths, however, and nobody really knows if there are long-term dangers. Now several human rights organizations are asking police to stop using them until further research is done.

A **Taser** looks like a gun. Instead of bullets, it shoots 50,000 volts of electricity. The current comes from batteries, and a nitrogen cartridge supplies power for the shot. When an officer pulls the trigger, the Taser shoots two barbs that are like small fishhooks. They are attached to the end of copper wires, and they can hit a person 21 feet away.

1. What are two ways that **Tasers** are safer than guns?

_____

_____

2. What questions still linger about **Tasers**?

_____

_____

3. What was the author's purpose for writing about the **Taser**?

_____

_____

Fluency: The words in the two sentences are all connected. The sentences are also missing punctuation and capitalization. Draw slash marks (/) between the words. Then rewrite the sentence, filling in the punctuation and capitalization.

1. theshockisshortbutpowerful

_____

ASSESSMENT

2. mostpeopleagreethattaserscanhelppolice

_____

_____

Fluency: Read the three sentences below. Imagine where you would pause within each sentence as you read it aloud. Draw a slash (/) mark between the phrases where you would pause. The first slash is done.

3. The Taser/is not the first weapon to shoot an electric current.

4. It is not clear when it is appropriate to use a Taser.

5. The Taser shoots two little hooks at the end of copper wires.

Vocabulary: Based on what you have learned in this lesson, match the following words with their definitions. Write the letter of the definition on the blank in front of the word it defines.

1. _____ effect

2. _____ medicinal

3. _____ police

4. _____ controversy

5. _____ long-term

6. _____ politician

7. _____ medic

8. _____ suspects

9. _____ metropolis

10. _____ appeal

A. a doctor working in a war zone

B. something with a bad taste

C. a city

D. people thought to be guilty

E. a disagreement about something

F. an outcome or result

G. someone who enforces the law

H. someone elected to work for government

I. an attraction

J. lasting a long period of time

Name _____ Date _____

ANTICIPATION GUIDE

Directions: <u>Before</u> you read the article "Space Is Filling With Junk," read the statements below. If you agree with a statement, put a check on the line. Otherwise, leave it blank.

_____ **1.** Outer space is too big to worry about old satellites.

_____ **2.** If outer space is polluted, it can be cleaned up easily.

_____ **3.** Pollution in outer space is a problem for all countries.

Once you have checked the statements above, tell why you agreed or disagreed with each statement in the section below.

1. _____

_____

2. _____

_____

3. _____

_____

In the box below, draw a picture of what you think this article is about.

"Space Is Filling With Junk"

What's Happening
IN THE USA?

By Lawrence Gable
© 2010 What's Happening Publications

Subject: Global Issues

The Soviet Union launched its satellite *Sputnik* in October 1957. Since then space has become more crowded. Unfortunately much of what orbits Earth now is junk.

As a result of space exploration, space debris now circles the planet. The objects are as large as rocket engines and as small as nuts and bolts. Astronauts also have lost things like coffee cups and a camera.

Space junk presents a danger. Most objects travel in "low orbit" 500–1,200 miles above Earth. They reach a speed of 22,300 miles per hour, so even the smallest objects can damage a spacecraft. Already they have dented the space shuttle and other spacecraft. In 1983 a speck of paint cracked the space shuttle's windshield.

The National Aeronautics and Space Administration (NASA) began to worry about space junk several decades ago. It watches anything at least 10 cm in diameter. There are more than 18,000 such objects, including about 850 working satellites. NASA believes that there are more than 100,000 pieces of junk 1–10 cm in diameter, and tens of millions smaller than that.

Low orbit space also has many satellites that no longer work. They stay in orbit for years, then fall into Earth's atmosphere and burn up. Now satellite owners try to move them out of the way. They send some into high orbit, where it is not crowded. They send others into Earth's atmosphere to burn up.

Satellites are big business. Ideally the owner uses the last bit of fuel to send a satellite into high orbit. If the company waits too long, the satellite runs out of fuel. Then it orbits as junk for about three years

before it falls and burns up. If the company sends the satellite into high orbit too soon, it loses time when the satellite could be earning money.

Certain locations in space are especially crowded. Some satellites must keep the same location over Earth, so they travel at the same speed that Earth turns. Those locations are getting more crowded.

A collision costs money and creates more debris. Only a few known collisions between two satellites have ever occurred, but the risk is growing.

In 2007 China created the most space junk ever. It used a missile to destroy an old weather satellite. That explosion created 2,300 pieces of debris larger than 4 cm in diameter, more than 35,000 pieces 1–4 cm in diameter, and a million pieces smaller than that. The international space community complained about the debris. Some nations complained that China just wanted to test its anti-satellite weapons.

In February 2008 the U.S. also shot down one of its own spy satellites. It would have fallen out of orbit in March. Most of it would have burnt up, but officials said that its rocket fuel could have landed and harmed people. Critics think that the U.S. really wanted to destroy secret photo equipment. China and Russia fear that the U.S. was just testing its anti-satellite weapons. No matter the reason, it caused more space junk.

Humans used to treat Earth's environment as dumping grounds for trash and pollution. Slowly they are learning to care for it. Now they also are learning that their actions affect space that once seemed so distant.

REACTION GUIDE

Directions: Now that you have read "Space Is Filling with Junk," reread the statements below. Then think about how the author would feel about these statements. If you think the author would agree, put a check on the line before the number. Then, below the statement, copy the words, phrases, or sentences in the article that tell you the author's real views.

_____ **1.** Outer space is too big to worry about old satellites.

Article notes: _____

_____

_____

_____ **2.** If outer space is polluted, it can be cleaned up easily.

Article notes: _____

_____

_____

_____ **3.** Cleaning up space is every country's problem.

Article notes: _____

_____

_____

PREDICTING ABC's

Directions: The article you are going to read is about "outer space." See how many boxes you can fill in below with words about outer space. For example, put the word "planet" in the P–R box. Try to put at least one word in every box.

A–C	D–F	G–I
J–L	**M–O**	**P–R**
S–T	**U–V**	**W–Z**

TIME MY READ # 1

Directions: With a partner, you will see how many words you can read correctly in 45 seconds. As you read, your partner will put an "X" through any word read incorrectly. Then your partner will read while you keep score. When you have both read, trade your books or papers. Count the total number of words you read correctly. Write this score at the bottom of your page.

WORD COUNT

debris dumping exploration satellites burnt travel engines distant	8
orbits explosion diameter atmosphere operators dented pieces fallen	16
fuel objects location missile functioned collision astronauts NASA	24
debris dumping exploration satellites burnt travel engines distant	32
orbits explosion diameter atmosphere operators dented pieces fallen	40
fuel objects location missile functioned collision astronauts NASA	48
debris dumping exploration satellites burnt travel engines distant	56
orbits explosion diameter atmosphere operators dented pieces fallen	64
fuel objects location missile functioned collision astronauts NASA	72
debris dumping exploration satellites burnt travel engines distant	80

Number of words read correctly _____.

ECHO READING

Directions: Your teacher will read aloud the text below. Listen carefully. Draw lines under the words he or she groups together. The first sentence has been done for you.

Space junk presents a danger to spacecraft and to humans in them. Most objects travel in "low orbit" 500–1,200 miles above Earth. They reach a speed of 22,300 miles per hour, so even the smallest bits of debris can damage a spacecraft. The space shuttle and other spacecraft have gotten dents from collisions. In 1983 a speck of paint cracked the space shuttle's windshield.

Certain locations in space are especially crowded. Some satellites must keep the same location over Earth, so they travel at the same speed that Earth turns. As more satellites go into space, those locations are getting more crowded. A collision costs money and creates more debris. Although only three known collisions between two satellites have ever occurred, the risk is growing all the time.

GET A CONTEXT CLUE

Directions: Below are sentences from "Space Is Filling With Junk." Read the sentence. Look back in the article and read the paragraph the sentence is in. Circle what you think is the best answer to each question.

"Unfortunately, much of what *orbits* the earth now is junk."

1. The word "orbits" means:

   A. burns
   B. pollutes
   C. goes around
   D. rotates

"As a result of space exploration, space *debris* now circles the planet."

2. "Debris" is best defined as:

   A. trash
   B. useful tools
   C. rocks
   D. building materials

"Low orbit space also has many *satellites* that no longer work."

3. The word "satellites" has to do with:

   A. objects sent to space
   B. other places for meeting
   C. telephone lines
   D. radio

"There are more than *18,000* such objects, including about 850 working satellites."

4. The correct way to say "18,000" is:

   A. one thousand eight hundred
   B. eighteen thousand and zero
   C. one hundred eighty thousand
   D. eighteen thousand

"Certain *locations* in space are especially crowded."

5. The word "locations" means:

   A. people
   B. types
   C. space ships
   D. places

"The *international* space community complained about the debris."

6. The word "international" means:

   A. from one country
   B. a group of people trying to solve a problem
   C. from many countries
   D. Americans

Name _____ Date _____

WORD MAP

Directions: Follow the directions to map the word in the box below.

debris

List 2 more words that mean the same.

List 2 more examples.

List 2 opposites or non-examples.

junk

Broken trees after a storm

treasure

Draw a picture below to help you remember the meaning.

Write a definition IN YOUR OWN WORDS.

LOOK WHO'S TALKING

Directions: Below are references from "Space Is Filling With Junk." Number each paragraph. Look back in the article and re-read the paragraph in which you find the reference. Circle what you think is the best answer to each question.

1. **In the third paragraph, the word "they" best refers to:**

   A. the junk
   B. nuts and bolts
   C. satellites
   D. the smallest objects

2. **In paragraph four, the word "it" refers to:**

   A. the objects
   B. the pieces
   C. the NASA agency
   D. the shuttle

3. **In paragraph five, the word "them" refers to:**

   A. the satellites
   B. the Earth
   C. the debris
   D. the owners

4. **In paragraph six, in the phrase "it loses time when the satellite could be earning money," the word "it" refers to:**

   A. the satellites
   B. the debris
   C. the people
   D. the company

5. **In paragraph seven in the last sentence, the word "those" refers to:**

   A. where the satellites are placed
   B. where the satellites collide
   C. where the satellites crash
   D. the satellite's speed

6. **In paragraph nine, the final sentence reads, "No matter the reason, it caused more space junk." The word "it" refers to:**

   A. the spy satellite
   B. the photo equipment
   C. shooting down the satellite
   D. the space station

HOW'S IT ORGANIZED?

This article is organized as *a problem that needs solving.*

Directions: Answer these questions in the spaces at the bottom.

1. What is the problem?

2. What is causing the problem?

3. Who has been worried about the problem for decades?

4. How did China increase the problem?

5. What has the U.S. done to make the problem worse?

6. What solutions are recommended or tried?

7. Are there new problems because of the solutions?

Answers:

1.	
2.	
3.	
4.	
5.	
6.	
7.	

IS THAT A FACT?

Directions: Read the definitions of a <u>fact</u> and an <u>inference</u> below. Then read the paragraph that follows. At the bottom of the page, write an "F" on the blank if a sentence is a fact. Write an "I" if the sentence is an inference. Use the following definitions:

<u>Fact</u> – a statement that can be proven to be true from the article.

<u>Inference</u> – a guess as to what MIGHT be true.

"On February 20, the United States shot down a spy satellite. It had been in orbit since December of 2006, but had never functioned properly. The satellite would have fallen out of orbit in March. Most of it would have burnt up, but officials said that its 1,000 pounds of rocket fuel could have landed in a populated area and harmed people. Critics suggest that the U.S. really wanted to destroy secret photo equipment. No matter the reason, it certainly caused more space junk."

_____ **1.** The U.S. had to shoot down their satellite.

_____ **2.** Shooting down the satellite created more space junk.

_____ **3.** The U.S. did not handle the situation of their broken satellite in the best way.

_____ **4.** The satellite probably would not have hurt anyone.

_____ **5.** The satellite was not built correctly.

MAKE A SPACE

Directions: Below are sentences that are missing punctuation and capitalization. First, draw slash marks (/) between the words. Then rewrite each sentence in the space below it, filling in the missing punctuation and capitalization.

Example:

space/debris/is/any/human/made/object/in/orbit/that/no/longer/

serves/a/useful/purpose

Space debris is any human made object in orbit that no longer serves a useful purpose.

1. spacejunkpresentsadangertospacecraftandtohumansinthem

_____

_____

2. theystayinorbitforyearsbeforetheyfinallyfallintoearthsatmosphereandburnup

_____

_____

3. certainlocationsinspaceareespeciallycrowded

_____

_____

4. humansusedtotreatearthslandwaterandairasdumpinggroundsfortrashandpollution

_____

_____

Name _____ Date _____

TIME MY READ # 2

Directions: With a partner, you will see how many words you can read correctly in 45 seconds. As you read, your partner will put an "X" through any word read incorrectly. Then your partner will read while you keep score. When you have both read, trade your books or papers. Count the total number of words you read correctly. Write this score at the bottom of your page.

WORD COUNT

debris dumping exploration satellites burnt travel engines distant	8
orbits explosion diameter atmosphere operators dented pieces fallen	16
fuel objects location missile functioned collision astronauts NASA	24
debris dumping exploration satellites burnt travel engines distant	32
orbits explosion diameter atmosphere operators dented pieces fallen	40
fuel objects location missile functioned collision astronauts NASA	48
debris dumping exploration satellites burnt travel engines distant	56
orbits explosion diameter atmosphere operators dented pieces fallen	64
fuel objects location missile functioned collision astronauts NASA	72
debris dumping exploration satellites burnt travel engines distant	80

Number of words read correctly _____. Is the score higher

than it was in Time My Read #1? _____

WORD PARTS

Directions: Read the definitions below. Then draw a spaceship as it orbits on the left orbital path. Show the spaceship shooting at space junk on the right orbital path.

1. **orb** – (noun) a round object; a circle or ball.

2. **orbit** – (noun) a path that circles around something else.

3. **to orbit** – (verb) to move around something.

4. **orbital** – (adjective) a word to describe the path of something moving around something else.

Orbital Path

Directions: The Latin root "loc" means *place*. Read the sentences below. Using the clues in the sentences, write a definition for each underlined word that begins with "loc."

1. Space junk is not a <u>local</u> problem in America; it is a problem for every country in the world.

2. Space junk can fall on any <u>locality</u> on earth—land or sea.

3. Certain <u>locations</u> in space are very crowded with junk.

4. The space shuttle needs to <u>locate</u> space junk in its way.

SUMMARIZING ABC's

Directions: Now that you've read the article on space junk, see how many words you can fill in the boxes below.

A–C	D–F	G–I
J–L	**M–O**	**P–R**
S–T	**U–V**	**W–Z**

SENTENCE SUMMARIES

Directions: Below are 4 key words from the article "Space Is Filling with Junk." Your job is to summarize, or restate, what you've learned in this article by using these 4 words or phrases in two sentences. Then, as a challenge, try to use all 4 words or phrases in one sentence to restate the article.

FOUR KEY WORDS OR PHRASES

debris   satellite(s)

orbit   collision

Sentence Summaries:

1. _____

_____

2. _____

_____

Challenge Summary (All 4 words or phrases in one sentence!)

1. _____

_____

_____

TAKE A STAND

Directions: People often have different feelings, or opinions, about the same thing. A "debate" is when people argue their different ideas. A good, persuasive argument has the following:

Facts – statements that can be proven to be true.

Statistics – research from a scientific study that uses numbers.

Examples – stories from the world that support an opinion.

You and a partner are going to debate two of your other classmates. The topic you are going to debate is the following:

Pollution in outer space is a problem for all countries.

Decide whether you agree or disagree with this statement.
Then answer these questions in order to win your debate.

1. What are your 2 strongest points to persuade the other side?
(You can do Internet research to include facts, statistics, and examples.)

A. _____

B. _____

2. What will the other side say to argue against point A?

_____

_____

3. What will the other side say to argue against point B?

_____

_____

4. What will you say to prove the other side's arguments are wrong?

_____

_____

Name _____ Date _____

Comprehension: Answer the questions about the passage below.

Space junk presents a danger to spacecraft and to humans in them. Most objects travel in a "low orbit" 500 – 1,200 miles above the Earth. They reach a speed of 22,300 miles per hour, so even the smallest bits of debris can damage a spacecraft. The space shuttle and other spacecraft have gotten dents from collisions. In 1993 a speck of paint cracked the space shuttle's windshield.

Certain locations in space are especially crowded. Some satellites must keep the same location over Earth, so they travel at the same speed that Earth turns. As more satellites go into space, those places are getting more crowded. Collisions cost money and create more debris. Although only three known collisions between two satellites have ever occurred, the risk is growing all the time.

1. Why should astronauts in spacecraft worry about space junk?

_____

_____

2. Why would a satellite travel at the same speed as the Earth?

_____

_____

3. Why don't scientists just blow up old satellites in outer space?

_____

_____

Fluency: The words in the two sentences are all connected. The sentences are also missing punctuation and capitalization. Draw slash marks (/) between the words. Then rewrite the sentence, filling in the punctuation and capitalization.

1. certainlocationsinspaceareespeciallycrowded

_____

_____

ASSESSMENT

2. spacejunkpresentsadangertospacecraftandtohumansinthem

_____

_____

Fluency: Read the three sentences below. Imagine where you would pause within each sentence as you read it aloud. Draw a slash (/) mark between the phrases where you would pause. The first slash is done.

3. On February 20 / the U.S. shot down a spy satellite.

4. As a result of space exploration space debris now circles the planet.

5. A collision costs money and creates more debris.

Vocabulary: Based on what you have learned in this lesson, match the following words with their definitions. Write the letter of the definition on the blank in front of the word it defines.

1. _____ debris   **A.** a round object; a ball

2. _____ orbit   **B.** to find where something is

3. _____ satellite   **C.** trash or junk left after a crash

4. _____ international   **D.** how something worked

5. _____ location   **E.** to move around something

6. _____ orb   **F.** nearby, in the area

7. _____ locate   **G.** an object sent into space

8. _____ fragile   **H.** a group involving several countries

9. _____ functioned   **I.** a place

10. _____ local   **J.** easily broken or ruined

Name _____ Date _____

ANTICIPATION GUIDE

Directions: <u>Before</u> you read the article "Concussions Have Long-Term Effects," read the statements below. If you agree with a statement, put a check on the line. Otherwise, leave it blank.

_____ **1.** Athletes understand the risk of injury when they play sports.

_____ **2.** The National Football League can't be responsible for a player's medical

problems.

_____ **3.** Injured players should be taken care of by their team.

Once you have checked the statements above, tell why you agreed or disagreed with each statement in the section below.

1. _____

_____

2. _____

_____

3. _____

_____

In the box below, draw a picture of what you think this article is about.

What's Happening
IN THE USA?

By Lawrence Gable
© 2010 What's Happening Publications

Subject: Sports

The National Football League (NFL) ends its season every year with the Super Bowl, one of the biggest days in American sport. However, the NFL also is having to face an ugly problem. Many players suffer concussions that destroy their lives after they retire.

A concussion starts with a blow to the head. The brain crashes into the skull, and that interrupts the brain's normal functions. The flow of blood to the brain slows. Brain cells lose their energy, and so does the person.

It is not always easy to know that a player has had a concussion. Athletes often do not report concussions to medical staff. Unfortunately, having suffered a concussion increases the chances of getting another one. Multiple concussions also increase the risk of long-term brain damage.

The brain has many functions, so a concussion causes many symptoms. Some concussions can cause a person to lose consciousness. Most cause players to react slowly, both physically and mentally. They are confused, lose memory and cannot concentrate. They can suffer headaches, nausea, slurred speech and blurred vision.

Lots of sports involve contact, but football players suffer repeated blows to the head. After a tough hit, players can get a vacant look in their eyes or cannot gain their balance. Players in the NFL call it getting "dinged." Brain experts do not like that term though, because it fails to recognize the seriousness of the injury.

Recovering from concussions requires time. Symptoms usually last one to ten days, but they can last weeks or months. During that time athletes need to avoid physical contact, because the brain easily could suffer worse, even permanent, injury. Most athletes can recover completely if they give their brains time to heal. They should not play again that day, but NFL coaches sent about half of them back into the game.

In 1994 the NFL began to study concussions. However, its committee did not include experts on brain injuries. The committee has failed to recognize the problems. It said that returning to play did not involve an increased risk of a second injury. It also reported that multiple concussions did not cause long-term damage. Criticism from doctors and retired players finally forced the chairman to resign.

Many retired players are showing the effects of multiple concussions. They are suffering from memory loss and depression. Brain experts studied 595 players who had suffered three or more concussions. Just over 20 percent of them had depression, which is three times the rate of other players. These mental and emotional problems leave retired players, even young ones, unable to lead normal lives.

In 2009 doctors announced a new finding. They had examined the brains of six former NFL players who had died by age 50. All six players had had a rare brain disease. Blows to the head cause it, and it results in dementia and other long-term brain problems in people in their 40s and 50s.

Football players understand that they can get concussions. Former players who are suffering, and whose lives are ruined, just want the NFL to face the problem. They also want players to understand that problems can last longer than the glory of the game.

"Concussions Have Long-Term Effects"

REACTION GUIDE

Directions: <u>Now that you have read</u> "Concussions Have Long-Term Effects," reread the statements below. Then think about how the author would feel about these statements. If you think the author would agree, put a check on the line before the number. Then, below the statement, copy the words, phrases, or sentences in the article that tell you the author's real views.

_____ **1.** Athletes understand the risk of injury when they play sports.

Article notes: _____

_____

_____

_____ **2.** The National Football League can't be responsible for a player's medical

problems.

Article notes: _____

_____

_____

_____ **3.** Injured players should be taken care of by their team.

Article notes: _____

_____

_____

WORDSTORM

Directions: It's good to know more than just the dictionary definition of a word. A wordstorm lets you write down information that helps you understand what a word means, how it's related to other words, and how to use it in different ways.

What is the word?

concussion
_____

Copy a sentence from the text in which the word is used:

_____

_____

What are some other words or phrases that mean the same thing?

_____

What are three things people might do to get a concussion?

1. _____ 2. _____ 3. _____

Name three people who would likely use this word other than

teachers.

1. _____ 2. _____ 3. _____

Draw a picture that reminds you of the word "concussion" below:

TIME MY READ # 1

Directions: With a partner, you will see how many words you can read correctly in 45 seconds. As you read, your partner will put an "X" through any word read incorrectly. Then your partner will read while you keep score. When you have both read, trade your books or papers. Count the total number of words you read correctly. Write this score at the bottom of your page.

WORD COUNT

concussions symptoms interrupts nausea confused vacant repeated committee	8
criticism report repeated serious injury experts physical depression	16
resign retired increases disease evidence suffered athletes chairman	24
concussions symptoms interrupts nausea confused vacant repeated committee	32
criticism report repeated serious injury experts physical depression	40
resign retired increases disease evidence suffered athletes chairman	48
concussions symptoms interrupts nausea confused vacant repeated committee	56
criticism report repeated serious injury experts physical depression	64
resign retired increases disease evidence suffered athletes chairman	72
consciousness symptoms interrupts nausea confused vacant repeated committee	80

Number of words read correctly _____.

ECHO READING

Directions: When you read, you should make breaks between groups of words. As the teacher reads each phrase, repeat aloud what was read and underline that phrase. Then you will read the whole sentence aloud together. The first sentence has been underlined for you.

Since the brain has countless functions, the symptoms vary and last varying lengths of time. Some concussions can cause a person to lose consciousness. Most, though, cause players to react slowly, both physically and mentally. They are confused, lose memory, and cannot concentrate. They misunderstand signals, and they do not know where they are or what the score is. They can suffer headaches, nausea, slurred speech, ringing in the ears, and blurred vision.

Recovering from a concussion requires time. After a concussion, symptoms usually last 24 hours to 10 days. However, they also can last weeks or months. During that time athletes need to avoid physical contact, because their brain easily could suffer worse, even permanent injury. Most athletes can recover completely if they give their brains time to heal. Coaches should certainly not allow them to play again that same day.

GET A CONTEXT CLUE

Directions: Below are sentences from "Concussions Have Long-Term Effects." Read the sentence. Look back in the article and read the paragraph the sentence is in. Then circle what you think is the best answer to each question.

"The brain crashes into the skull and that interrupts the brain's normal *functions*."

1. The word "functions" means:

    A. blood

    B. role or purpose

    C. water

    D. skull

"Athletes often do not *report* concussions to medical staff."

2. The word "report" means:

    A. lie about

    B. talk about

    C. allow

    D. imagine

"The brain has many functions so a concussion causes many *symptoms*."

3. The word "symptoms" means:

    A. effects

    B. dreams

    C. goals

    D. ideas

"It also reported that *multiple* concussions did not cause long-term brain damage."

4. The word "multiple" means:

    A. many

    B. a few

    C. once or twice

    D. none

"In 2009 doctors *announced* a new finding."

5. The word "announced" means:

    A. spoke openly about

    B. denied

    C. supported

    D. covered up

"Former players who are suffering, and whose lives are ruined, just want the NFL to *face* the problem."

6. Another way to say "face" is:

    A. ignore

    B. argue about

    C. forget

    D. deal with

WORD CHOICE

Directions: As you read this piece, you will find blanks for missing words. Three words are listed after the blank. One of these is correct. <u>Read the rest of the sentence past the blank to figure out which is the correct word</u>. Write it in the blank.

In 1994 the NFL formed a committee to study concussions. However, none of the _____ (member, members, membering) was an expert on brain _____ (injuring, injuries, injury). The committee has _____ (failed, failing, failure) to acknowledge the problems. In 2005 the committee _____ (concluded, conclusion, concluding) that returning to play did not _____ (involvement, involved, involve) significant risk of injury. It also _____ (reporting, reporter, reported) that there _____ (would, wasn't, weren't) evidence of long-term effects from multiple concussions. Criticism from retired doctors and players finally _____ (forced, force, forcing) the chairman to quit.

Football _____ (was, is, isn't) a contact sport, and players _____ (understand, understanding, understood) that they can _____ (got, getting, get) concussions. Former players who are _____ (suffered, suffering, suffer) and whose lives _____ (is, are, was) ruined, just want the NFL to _____ (acknowledging, acknowledged, acknowledge) the problem. They also want players to understand that problems can last longer than the glory of the game.

LOOK WHO'S TALKING

Directions: Below are references from "Concussions Have Long-Term Effects." Number each paragraph. Look back in the article and re-read the paragraph in which you find the reference. Circle what you think is the best answer to each question.

1. In the second paragraph, the word "their" best refers to:

A. the NFL
B. the brain
C. the players
D. the cells

2. In paragraph four, the word "they" is used several times to best refer to:

A. the brain
B. the concussions
C. the person
D. the players

3. In paragraph seven, the word "its" refers to:

A. the brain
B. the NFL
C. the committee
D. the league

4. In paragraph eight, the word "them" refers to:

A. the brain experts
B. the players
C. the problems
D. the young ones

5. In paragraph nine the word "it" refers to:

A. the concussions
B. the brains
C. the players
D. the brain disease

6. In paragraph ten the word "they" refers to:

A. the former players
B. the young players
C. problems
D. the concussions

Name _____ Date _____

Directions: Read the key words on the left side of the chart below. Then add notes that answer the question in parentheses under the key word.

concussion (Why?)	
effects on brain (How?)	
1994 study (What?)	
Chairman resigns (Why?)	
2009 study (What?)	

"Concussions Have Long-Term Effects"

IS THAT A FACT?

Directions: Read the definitions of a <u>fact</u> and an <u>inference</u> below. Then read the paragraph that follows. At the bottom of the page, write an "F" on the blank if a sentence is a fact or an "I" if it is an inference. Use the following definitions:

Fact – a statement that can be proven to be true from the article.

Inference – a guess as to what MIGHT be true.

> "Now many retired football players are showing the effects of multiple concussions. They are suffering from memory loss, dementia, and depression. Brain experts studied 595 players who had suffered three or more concussions. Just over 20 percent of them had depression, which is three times the rate of other players. These mental and emotional problems leave retired players, even young ones, unable to lead normal lives. They cannot work or keep their marriages together."

_____ **1.** Football can be dangerous to your health.

_____ **2.** Many former players have trouble leading normal lives.

_____ **3.** Doctors would not recommend playing football.

_____ **4.** Players who have concussions suffer loss of memory.

_____ **5.** Retired football players have many arguments with their spouses.

MAKE A SPACE

Directions: Below are sentences that are missing punctuation and capitalization. First, draw slash marks (/) between the words. Then rewrite each sentence in the space below it, filling in the missing punctuation and capitalization.

Example:

lots/of/sports/involve/contact/but/football/players/suffer/repeated/

blows/to/the/head

Lots of sports involve contact, but football players suffer repeated

blows to the head.

1. recoveringfromconcussionsrequirestime

_____

_____

2. nowmanyretiredplayersareshowingtheeffectsofmultipleconcussions

_____

_____

3. playerswhoaresufferingwanttheleaguetoacknowledgetheproblem

_____

_____

4. footballisacontactsportandplayersunderstandtheycangetaconcussion

_____

_____

"Concussions Have Long-Term Effects"

TIME MY READ # 2

Directions: With a partner, you will see how many words you can read correctly in 45 seconds. As you read, your partner will put an "X" through any word read incorrectly. Then your partner will read while you keep score. When you have both read, trade your books or papers. Count the total number of words you read correctly. Write this score at the bottom of your page.

WORD COUNT

concussions symptoms interrupts nausea confused vacant repeated committee	8
criticism report repeated serious injury experts physical depression	16
resign retired increases disease evidence suffered athletes chairman	24
concussions symptoms interrupts nausea confused vacant repeated committee	32
criticism report repeated serious injury experts physical depression	40
resign retired increases disease evidence suffered athletes chairman	48
concussions symptoms interrupts nausea confused vacant repeated committee	56
criticism report repeated serious injury experts physical depression	64
resign retired increases disease evidence suffered athletes chairman	72
consciousness symptoms interrupts nausea confused vacant repeated committee	80

Number of words read correctly _____. Is the score higher than it was in

Time My Read #1? _____

WORD PARTS

Directions: A **base word** is a word that can stand alone. A **prefix** is a word part added to the beginning of a base word. For example, in the word **misspeak, speak** is the base word and **mis-** is the prefix added at the beginning. The prefix **mis-** means "wrong" or "wrongly." *Misspeak* means to say something wrongly or incorrectly. Write a definition on the line for the words below. Do <u>not</u> use the base word in the definition. If you don't know the base word, such as *deed* in "misdeed," look it up in a dictionary or ask a partner.

1. misunderstand – _____

2. misplace – _____

3. mistrust – _____

4. misjudge – _____

5. misfire – _____

6. misbehave – _____

7. mishandle – _____

8. misuse – _____

9. mistaken – _____

10. misinform – _____

11. misfit – _____

12. mismanage – _____

13. mistrial – _____

14. mislead – _____

15. misdeed – _____

"Concussions Have Long-Term Effects"

CONCUSSION WORD PUZZLE

Directions: Complete the crossword puzzle.

Across

2 to act in a way that is incorrect
3 a court trial that is done incorrectly
7 a purpose or role
8 to decide or evaluate wrongly
9 talk about or inform

Down

1 an injury to the brain caused by a hard hit
2 to tell someone the wrong information
4 said or stated aloud
5 an effect
6 more than one; many

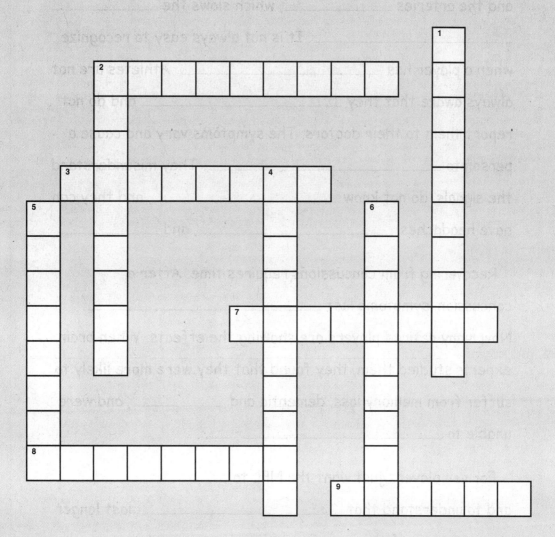

Word List

CONCUSSION	MISBEHAVE	REPORT	MULTIPLE	MISJUDGE
MISINFORM	MISTRIAL	FUNCTION	ANNOUNCED	SYMPTOM

Name _____ Date _____

WRITING FRAME

Directions: Below is a writing frame. Use your knowledge and information from the article to complete the frame below.

The NFL is having to face an ugly problem. May players suffer concussions that destroy their lives after they retire. A concussion starts with _____, and the arteries _____, which slows the _____ _____. It is not always easy to recognize when a player has _____. Athletes are not always aware that they _____ and do not report them to their doctors. The symptoms vary and cause a person to _____. They misunderstand the signals, do not know _____, and they can have headaches, _____, _____, and _____.

Recovering from concussions requires time. After a concussion, symptoms last _____. Now many retired players are showing the effects. When brain experts studied them, they found that they were more likely to suffer from memory loss, dementia and _____, and were unable to _____.

Former players just want the NFL to _____ and to understand that _____ last longer than the glory of the game.

54   "Concussions Have Long-Term Effects"

TAKE A STAND

Directions: People often have different feelings, or opinions, about the same thing. A "debate" is when people argue their different ideas. A good, persuasive argument has the following:

Facts – statements that can be proven to be true.

Statistics – research from a scientific study that uses numbers.

Examples – stories from the world that support an opinion.

You and a partner are going to debate two of your other classmates. The topic you are going to debate is the following:

The NFL should care for retired injured players.

Decide whether you agree or disagree with this statement. Then answer these questions in order to win your debate.

1. What are your 2 strongest points to persuade the other side?
(You can do Internet research to include facts, statistics, and examples.)

A. _____

B. _____

2. What will the other side say to argue against point A?
_____
_____

3. What will the other side say to argue against point B?
_____
_____

4. What will you say to prove the other side's arguments are wrong?
_____
_____

ASSESSMENT

Comprehension: Answer the questions about the passage below.

Since the brain has countless functions, the symptoms of a concussion vary and last varying lengths of time. Some concussions can cause a person to lose consciousness. Most, though, cause players to react slowly, both physically and mentally. They are confused, lose memory, and cannot concentrate. They misunderstand signals, and they do not know where they are or what the score is. They can suffer headaches, nausea, slurred speech, ringing in the ears, and blurred vision.

After a concussion, symptoms usually last 24 hours to 10 days. However, they also can last weeks or months. During that time athletes need to avoid physical contact, because their brain easily could suffer worse, even permanent injury. Most athletes can recover completely if they give their brains time to heal. Coaches should certainly not allow them to play again that same day.

1. What problems do concussions cause?

_____

_____

2. What was the author's purpose for writing about concussions?

_____

_____

Fluency: The words in the two sentences are all connected. The sentences are also missing punctuation and capitalization. Draw slash (/) marks between the words. Then rewrite the sentence, filling in the punctuation and capitalization.

1. recoveringfromconcussionsrequirestime

_____

_____

2. lotsofsportsinvolvecontactbutfootballplayerssufferrepeatedblowstothehead

_____

_____

Fluency: Read the three sentences below. Imagine where you would pause within each sentence as you read it aloud. Draw a slash (/) mark between the phrases where you would pause. The first slash is done.

3. A concussion / starts with a blow to the head.

4. Once a player has gotten a concussion, his or her chances of getting another are increased.

5. Most athletes can recover if they give their brains time to heal.

Vocabulary: Based on what you have learned in this lesson, match the following words with their definitions. Write the letter of the definition on the blank in front of the word it defines.

1. _____ mistrial   **A.** to give information that is incorrect

2. _____ concussion   **B.** state or say aloud

3. _____ report   **C.** a purpose or role

4. _____ symptom   **D.** a court trial that is done wrongly

5. _____ misbehave   **E.** an effect

6. _____ function   **F.** to talk about or inform

7. _____ misinform   **G.** to decide or evaluate incorrectly

8. _____ announce   **H.** to act in a way that is not correct

9. _____ misjudge   **I.** more than one

10. _____ multiple   **J.** an injury to the brain caused by a hard hit

Name _____ Date _____

ANTICIPATION GUIDE

Directions: <u>Before</u> you read the article "Plastic Swirls in the Pacific," read the statements below. If you agree with a statement, put a check on the line. Otherwise, leave it blank.

_____ **1.** The Pacific Ocean is so big that trash is not a problem.

_____ **2.** The United States is responsible for keeping oceans clean.

_____ **3.** If the ocean gets polluted, it can eventually be cleaned up.

Once you have checked the statements above, tell why you agreed or disagreed with each statement in the section below.

1. _____

_____

2. _____

_____

3. _____

_____

In the box below, draw a picture of what you think this article is about.

_____

What's Happening
IN THE WORLD?

By Lawrence Gable
© 2010 What's Happening Publications

Subject: Environment

Plastic Swirls in the Pacific

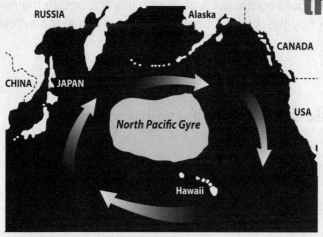

Plastic became popular in the 1950s. Since then a lot of plastic trash has gone into the oceans. In 1997 a sailor sailed through a remote part of the Pacific Ocean and found it covered with trash. At the time he said the plastic covered an area the size of Texas. Now it has grown to the size of Australia.

The area lies about 1,000 miles west of the U.S. mainland and 1,000 miles north of Hawaii. It is called the North Pacific Gyre. Now it also has unflattering names like "the garbage patch" and "the plastic soup." It forms the largest mass of trash on Earth. It stretches thousands of miles and 300 feet deep.

A sailor named Charles Moore discovered it. On his return from Hawaii to California he sailed through the North Pacific Gyre. Sailors rarely go there because for hundreds of miles there is no wind and the ocean's surface is smooth. It took him a week to cross it, and trash surrounded him the entire time.

Four Pacific currents bring the trash to that spot. They move in a clockwise pattern near Japan, up toward Alaska, down along North America, and south of Hawaii. The currents push two masses of water together, and where they meet the water circulates and sinks. That is why the area is called a gyre. Water swirls like water in a toilet that will not flush, and anything that floats stays on the surface.

Researchers have found all kinds of plastic things there. They find many plastic bags, bottles and containers. Large numbers of unusual things are floating there too, like umbrella handles, huge fishing nets, toolboxes and orange traffic cones.

Under normal circumstances the things that float are alive. The small animal life that other creatures feed on makes the gyre a fine hunting ground for seabirds. However, researchers have found almost none of those small floating animals.

Birds and fish mistake plastic for food. Experts estimate that it kills more than a million seabirds and 100,000 marine mammals every year. When researchers have opened up dead seabirds in the Pacific, they have found cigarette lighters, bottle caps and toothbrushes in their stomachs.

Most of what floats in the gyre is plastic. About one-fifth of it comes from ships and oil platforms. The rest comes from land, where it goes from storm drains into streams, and then into the ocean. The water's circulating motion finally pulls the trash from the coasts of Asia and North America into the "plastic soup."

The trash in the gyre does not form a solid mass. Much of it floats, but even more hangs suspended in the water. Sunlight makes plastic brittle, so it breaks into tiny pieces and even into a plastic dust. Researchers from the United Nations estimate that there are a million pieces of plastic per square mile. Most of them are only a few millimeters across.

About 90 per cent of all trash floating in the oceans is plastic. Cleaning up the gyre will be nearly impossible. It lies in international waters, so no single country will clean it up. For now people must handle plastic objects more responsibly. They can use less plastic packaging, recycle more plastic, and dispose of it properly so that it never reaches the ocean.

REACTION GUIDE

Directions: Now that you have read "Plastic Swirls in the Pacific," reread the statements below. Then think about how the author would feel about these statements. If you think the author would agree, put a check on the line before the number. Then, below the statement, copy the words, phrases, or sentences in the article that tell you the author's real views.

_____ **1.** The Pacific Ocean is so big that trash is not a problem.

Article notes: _____

_____

_____

_____ **2.** The United States is responsible for keeping oceans clean.

Article notes: _____

_____

_____

_____ **3.** If the ocean gets polluted, it can eventually be cleaned up.

Article notes: _____

_____

_____

PREDICTING ABC's

Directions: The article you are going to read is about "pollution in the ocean." See how many words you can fill in below about the ocean and what might make it dirty. For example, put the word "oil" in the M–O box. Try to put at least one word in every box.

A–C	D–F	G–I
J–L	**M–O**	**P–R**
S–T	**U–V**	**W–Z**

TIME MY READ # 1

Directions: With a partner, you will see how many words you can read correctly in 45 seconds. As you read, your partner will put an "X" through any word read incorrectly. Then your partner will read while you keep score. When you have both read, trade your books or papers. Count the total number of words you read correctly. Write this score at the bottom of your page.

WORD COUNT

remote gyre researchers current rarely mainland swirls circulates	8
creatures hunting surface plastic containers experts seabirds drains	16
unflattering wind floating unusual packaging brittle waters millimeters	24
remote gyre researchers current rarely mainland swirls circulates	32
creatures hunting surface plastic containers experts seabirds drains	40
unflattering wind floating unusual packaging brittle waters millimeters	48
remote gyre researchers current rarely mainland swirls circulates	56
creatures hunting surface plastic containers experts seabirds drains	64
unflattering wind floating unusual packaging brittle waters millimeters	72
remote gyre researchers current rarely mainland swirls circulates	80

Number of words read correctly _____.

ECHO READING

Directions: When you read, you should make breaks between groups of words. As the teacher reads each phrase, repeat aloud what was read and underline that phrase. Then you will read the whole sentence aloud together. The first sentence has been underlined for you.

The area lies about 1,000 miles west of the U.S. mainland and 1,000 miles north of Hawaii. It is called the North Pacific Gyre. Now it also has unflattering names like "the garbage patch" and "the plastic soup." It forms the largest mass of trash on Earth. It stretches thousands of miles and 300 feet deep.

A sailor named Charles Moore discovered it in 1997. On his return from Hawaii to California he sailed through the North Pacific Gyre. Sailors rarely go there because for hundreds of miles there is no wind and the ocean's surface is smooth. It took him a week to cross it, and trash surrounded him the entire time.

Most of what floats in the gyre is plastic. About one-fifth of it comes from ships and oil platforms. The rest comes from land, where it goes from storm drains into streams, and then into the ocean. The water's circulating motion finally pulls the trash from the coasts of Asia and North America into the "plastic soup."

GET A CONTEXT CLUE

Directions: Below are sentences from "Plastic Swirls in the Pacific." Read the sentence. Look back in the article and read the paragraph the sentence is in. Then circle what you think is the best answer to each question.

"It forms the largest *mass* of trash on Earth."

1. The word "mass" means:

    A. large collection of something
    B. pollution
    C. picture
    D. island

"Four Pacific *currents* bring the trash to that spot."

2. The word "current" is best described as

    A. the movement of water
    B. a bolt of electricity
    C. occurring at this moment
    D. electricity

"*Researchers* have found all kinds of plastic things there."

3. "Researchers" are best described as:

    A. people in government
    B. a group of people trying to solve a problem
    C. polluters
    D. people involved in shipping

"Under normal *circumstances* the things that float are alive."

4. The word "circumstances" means:

    A. places
    B. oceans
    C. events or conditions
    D. problems

"Sunlight makes plastic *brittle*, so it breaks into tiny pieces and even into plastic dust."

5. The word "brittle" means:

    A. thick
    B. strong
    C. breaks easily
    D. touch

"For now people must handle plastic objects more *responsibly*."

6. The word "responsibly" means:

    A. quickly
    B. with good judgment; reliably
    C. easily
    D. badly

WORD MAP

Directions: Follow the directions to map the word in the box below.

pollution

List 2 more words that mean the same.

List 2 more examples.

List 2 opposites or non-examples.

garbage

smog

clean air

Draw a picture below to help you remember the meaning.

Write a definition IN YOUR OWN WORDS.

LOOK WHO'S TALKING

Directions: Below are references from "Plastic Swirls in the Pacific." Number each paragraph. Look back in the article and re-read the paragraph in which you find the reference. Circle what you think is the best answer to each question.

1. In the first paragraph, the word "it" best refers to:

   A. the plastic
   B. the ocean
   C. a remote area
   D. the trash

2. In the third paragraph, in last sentence "it took him a week to cross it…" the first "it" refers to:

   A. the area
   B. the ocean
   C. the North Pacific
   D. the amount of time he took

3. In paragraph four, in the sentence, "the currents push two masses together where they meet…" the word "they" means

   A. the currents
   B. the trash
   C. the oceans
   D. the gyre

4. In paragraph seven the word "they" refers to:

   A. the plastic
   B. the seabirds
   C. the countries
   D. the researchers

5. In paragraph nine the word "estimate" refers to:

   A. the amount
   B. the size
   C. the currents
   D. the time

6. In paragraph ten, the word "they" refers to:

   A. the people
   B. the countries
   C. the plastic
   D. the gyre

Name _____ Date _____

This article is organized as *a problem that needs solving*.

Directions: Answer these questions in the spaces at the bottom.

1. What is the problem?

2. Who discovered the problem?

3. What is causing the problem in the Pacific Ocean?

4. What are the effects of the problem?

5. Is anyone trying to solve the problem? If yes, who?

6. Why is the floating plastic a hard problem to solve?

7. What solutions are recommended?

Answers:

1.	
2.	
3.	
4.	
5.	
6.	
7.	

IS THAT A FACT?

Directions: Read the definitions of a <u>fact</u> and an <u>inference</u> below. Then read the paragraph that follows. At the bottom of the page, write an "F" on the blank if a sentence is a fact or an "I" if it is an inference. Use the following definitions:

<u>Fact</u> – a statement that can be proven to be true from the article.

<u>Inference</u> – a guess as to what MIGHT be true.

> "Most of what floats in the gyre is plastic. About one-fifth of it comes from ships and oil platforms. The rest comes from land, where it goes from storm drains into streams, and then into the ocean. The water's circulating motion finally pulls the trash from the coasts of Asia and North America into the "plastic soup."

_____ **1.** Two of the largest polluters are Asia and North America.

_____ **2.** The ocean's current pulls the trash out to sea.

_____ **3.** People tend to be careless about how they dispose of trash.

_____ **4.** Most of the pollution comes from plastic.

_____ **5.** Some ships and oil platforms don't care about pollution.

_____ **6.** Since so many people drink water out of plastic bottles, the amount of trash in the Pacific gyre will only grow larger.

MAKE A SPACE

Directions: Below are sentences that are missing punctuation and capitalization. First, draw slash marks (/) between the words. Then rewrite each sentence in the space below it, filling in the missing punctuation and capitalization.

An example is provided:

eleven/years/ago/a/sailor/sailed/through/a/remote/part/of/
the/pacific/ocean

Eleven years ago a sailor sailed through a remote part of the
Pacific Ocean.

1. fourpacificcurrentsbringthetrashtothatspot

_____

2. researchershavefoundallkindsofplasticthingsdownthere

_____

3. thewaterscirculatingmotionfinallypullsthetrashfromthecoastsofasia
andnorthamericaintotheplasticsoup

_____

_____

4. about90percentofthetrashfloatingintheoceanisplastic

_____

_____

TIME MY READ # 2

Directions: With a partner, you will see how many words you can read correctly in 45 seconds. As you read, your partner will put an "X" through any word read incorrectly. Then your partner will read while you keep score. When you have both read, trade your books or papers. Count the total number of words you read correctly. Write this score at the bottom of your page.

WORD COUNT

remote gyre researchers current rarely mainland swirls circulates	8
creatures hunting surface plastic containers experts seabirds drains	16
unflattering wind floating unusual packaging brittle waters millimeters	24
remote gyre researchers current rarely mainland swirls circulates	32
creatures hunting surface plastic containers experts seabirds drains	40
unflattering wind floating unusual packaging brittle waters millimeters	48
remote gyre researchers current rarely mainland swirls circulates	56
creatures hunting surface plastic containers experts seabirds drains	64
unflattering wind floating unusual packaging brittle waters millimeters	72
remote gyre researchers current rarely mainland swirls circulates	80

Number of words read correctly _____. Is the score higher

than it was in Time My Read #1?_____

WORD PARTS

Directions: The Latin root "circulus" means *circle*. Read the definitions below. Then draw a picture of what each word means.

1. **circle** – (noun) a ring, a continuous curve that ends where it begins.

2. **circus** – (noun) a group of performers with clowns and animals who travel and usually perform under a large tent.

3. **circulate** – (verb) to move from place to place or from person to person.

4. **circumference** – (noun) the distance around something.

circle	circulate	circus	circumference

Directions: The Latin root "marinus" means *sea* or *ocean*. Read the sentences below. Then write a definition for the **bold** word.

1. The **marines** normally travel on ships to the places where they will fight for their country.

2. The city of Norfolk is a large port having many **maritime** businesses, such as shipbuilding, fishing, sail makers, and seafood restaurants.

3. There were many expensive boats and yachts docked in the **marina**.

4. Some examples of **marine** animals would be fish, seals, and whales.

SUMMARIZING ABC's

Directions: Now that you've read the article on the pollution in the Pacific Ocean, see how many words you can fill in the boxes below.

A–C	D–F	G–I
J–L	M–O	P–R
S–T	U–V	W–Z

"Plastic Swirls in the Pacific"

SENTENCE SUMMARIES

Directions: Below are 4 key words from the article "Plastic Swirls in the Pacific." Your job is to summarize, or restate, what you've learned in this article by using these 4 words or phrases in two sentences. Then, as a challenge, try to use all 4 words or phrases in one sentence to restate the article.

FOUR KEY WORDS OR PHRASES

gyre   currents

international   responsibility

Sentence Summaries:

1._____

_____

2._____

_____

Challenge Summary (All 4 words or phrases in one sentence!)

1._____

_____

_____

TAKE A STAND

Directions: People often have different feelings, or opinions, about the same thing. A "debate" is when people argue their different ideas. A good, persuasive argument has the following:

Facts – statements that can be proven to be true.

Statistics – research from a scientific study that uses numbers.

Examples – stories from the world that support an opinion.

You and a partner are going to debate two of your other classmates. The topic you are going to debate is the following:

> *The huge plastic gyre in the Pacific is everyone's problem.*

Decide whether you agree or disagree with this statement.
Then answer these questions in order to win your debate.

1. What are your 2 strongest points to persuade the other side?
   (You can do Internet research to include facts, statistics, and examples.)

A. _____

B. _____

2. What will the other side say to argue against point A?

_____

_____

3. What will the other side say to argue against point B?

_____

_____

4. What will you say to prove the other side's arguments are wrong?

_____

_____

ASSESSMENT

Comprehension: Answer the questions about the passage below.

   The area lies about 1,000 miles west of the U.S. mainland and 1,000 miles north of Hawaii. It is called the North Pacific Gyre. Now it also has unflattering names like "the garbage patch" and "the plastic soup." It forms the largest mass of trash on Earth. It stretches thousands of miles and 300 feet deep. Most of what floats in the gyre is plastic. About one–fifth of it comes from ships and oil platforms. The rest comes from land, where it goes from storm drains into streams, and then into the ocean. The water's circulating motion finally pulls the trash from the coasts of Asia and North America.

1. What are two causes of the plastic gyre?

_____

_____

2. Why might the plastic gyre be a tremendous problem?

_____

_____

3. What was the author's purpose for writing about the gyre?

_____

_____

Fluency: The words in the two sentences are all connected. The sentences are also missing punctuation and capitalization. Draw slash marks (/) between the words. Then rewrite the sentence, filling in the punctuation and capitalization.

1. thegyreresultsfromfourcurrentsthatpullthetrashtooneplace

_____

_____

ASSESSMENT

2. thegyreisininternationalwatersandnocountryacceptsresponsibility

_____

_____

Fluency: Read the three sentences below. Imagine where you would pause within each sentence as you read it aloud. Draw a slash (/) mark between the phrases where you would pause. The first slash is done.

3. Birds and fish / mistake the plastic for food.

4. It took him a week to cross the area, and the entire time he was surrounded by trash.

5. Although much of it floats even more hangs suspended in the water.

Vocabulary: Based on what you have learned in this lesson, match the following words with their definitions. Write the letter of the definition on the blank in front of the word it defines.

1. _____ circulate

2. _____ brittle

3. _____ marina

4. _____ pollution

5. _____ circumference

6. _____ responsibly

7. _____ current

8. _____ circle

9. _____ maritime

10. _____ marines

A. the distance around something

B. soldiers who travel aboard ships

C. harmful stuff put in the environment

D. a ring or continuous curve

E. breaks easily

F. having to do with the ocean or sea

G. to move from one place to another

H. a place to dock or store ships

I. the movement of water

J. with good judgment; reliably

Name _____ Date _____

ANTICIPATION GUIDE

Directions: <u>Before</u> you read the article "The Grammy Awards," read the statements below. If you agree with a statement, put a check on the line. Otherwise, leave it blank.

_____ **1.** Mostly only Americans watch the Grammy Awards.

_____ **2.** The Grammys reward the most popular musicians.

_____ **3.** The public really decides who wins a Grammy Award.

Once you have checked the statements above, tell why you agreed or disagreed with each statement in the section below.

1. _____

_____

2. _____

_____

3. _____

_____

In the box below, draw a picture of what you think this article is about.

What's Happening
IN THE USA?

By Lawrence Gable
© 2010 What's Happening Publications

Subject: Art

Every year the National Academy of Recording Arts and Sciences honors people in the music industry. Winners receive a statuette of an old record player, which was called a gramophone. The award is the "Grammy."

The National Academy, often called the Recording Academy, started in 1957. The city of Hollywood was creating a "Walk of Fame" on Hollywood Boulevard. It wanted to put the names of entertainers in stars in the sidewalk. It asked heads of five recording companies to suggest names. When they met, they also got the idea of an academy for the music industry.

They founded the Recording Academy that same year. It recognizes musical excellence and helps music makers. Some of its members are musicians, songwriters and music producers who create music. Others are company leaders, disc jockeys and business agents who promote the music.

A year later the Grammy was born. About 500 people attended the first award ceremony in 1958. Television did not broadcast the ceremony, and there were no musical performances. There were winners in 28 categories in musical fields like jazz, rhythm & blues and classical. The great jazz singer Ella Fitzgerald won two Grammys.

The Recording Academy received some criticism that first year. It centered around the exciting new field of music, rock & roll. Although singers like Elvis Presley and Bobby Darin already had become stars, there were no rock & roll awards. In fact, it was not until 1961 that "Best Rock & Roll Recording" became an award. Rock & roll categories

did not become permanent until 1979. Critics say that the Recording Academy also was slow to recognize new fields like heavy metal, hip-hop and rap.

The Academy's response is that the Grammys reward artistic excellence, not popularity. In that first year, for example, the wildly popular Frank Sinatra received twelve nominations. He won only one Grammy though. Over fifty years plenty of other popular artists never have won.

Nominations come from the Academy's members and from record companies. The recordings and music videos must have appeared before September 30. Members can make nominations in the four general categories ("Record of the Year," "Album of the Year," "Song of the Year" and "Best New Artist") and in nine of the 31 fields of music. The result is five finalists in all 110 categories.

Voting then takes place. The Recording Academy keeps the winners a secret. However, it sends the results to the company in Colorado that makes the statuettes. The company puts the winners' names on them and delivers them to the Academy in person.

In 1973 the Recording Academy also started a Grammy Hall of Fame. At first it was only for great artists and performances from before 1958. Now it honors those that are at least 25 years old. In 1990 the Recording Academy also started giving Legend Awards to legendary performers. More than a billion people around the world will watch the telecast of the ceremony. Music sales increase for the winners. Beyond that, they become part of the history of the music industry's highest award, the Grammy.

REACTION GUIDE

Directions: <u>Now that you have read</u> "The Grammy Awards," reread the statements below. Then think about how the author would feel about these statements. If you think the author would agree, put a check on the line before the number. Then, below the statement, copy the words, phrases, or sentences in the article that tell you the author's real views.

_____ **1.** Mostly only Americans watch the Grammy Awards.

Article notes: _____

_____

_____

_____ **2.** The Grammys reward the most popular musicians.

Article notes: _____

_____

_____

_____ **3.** The public really decides who wins a Grammy Award.

Article notes: _____

_____

_____

WORDSTORM

Directions: It's good to know more than just the dictionary definition of a word. A wordstorm lets you write down information that helps you understand what a word means, how it's related to other words, and how to use it in different ways.

What is the word?

excellence
_____

Copy the sentence from the text in which the word is used:

_____

_____

What are some other words or phrases that mean the same thing?

_____

What are three qualities that people have that create excellence?

1. _____ 2. _____ 3. _____

Name three people who would likely use this word other than teachers.

1. _____ 2. _____ 3. _____

Draw a picture that reminds you of the word "excellence" below:

TIME MY READ # 1

Directions: With a partner, you will see how many words you can read correctly in 45 seconds. As you read, your partner will put an "X" through any word read incorrectly. Then your partner will read while you keep score. When you have both read, trade your books or papers. Count the total number of words you read correctly. Write this score at the bottom of your page.

WORD COUNT

national industry statuette honor record player gramophone Grammy anniversary	8
academy recognize entertainers companies fame excellence broadcast finalists	16
legendary business agent award ceremony broadcast jazz rhythm & blues	24
national industry statuette honor record player gramophone Grammy anniversary	32
academy recognize entertainers companies fame excellence broadcast finalists	40
legendary business agent award ceremony broadcast jazz rhythm & blues	48
national industry statuette honor record player gramophone Grammy anniversary	56
academy recognize entertainers companies fame excellence broadcast finalists	64
legendary business agent award ceremony broadcast jazz rhythm & blues	72
national industry statuette honor record player gramophone Grammy anniversary	80

Number of words read correctly _____ .

ECHO READING

Directions: When you read, you should make breaks between groups of words. As the teacher reads each phrase, repeat aloud what was read and underline that phrase. Then you will read the whole sentence aloud together. The first sentence has been underlined for you.

The National Academy, often called the Recording Academy, started almost by accident. In 1957 the city of Hollywood was creating a "walk of fame" on Hollywood Boulevard. It wanted to put the names of entertainers in stars in the sidewalk. It asked five executives of recording companies to suggest names. When they met, they also came up with the idea of an academy for the music industry.

They founded the Recording Academy that same year. Its mission is to recognize musical excellence, help music makers, and ensure that music remains a key part of American culture. Its members represent both the creative side of the industry (musicians, song writers, and music producers) and the business side (company executives, disc jockeys, and business agents).

GET A CONTEXT CLUE

Directions: Below are sentences from "The Grammy Awards." Read the sentence. Look back in the article and read the paragraph the sentence is in. Then circle what you think is the best answer to each question.

"Winners receive a statuette of an old record player, which was called a *gramophone*."

1. A "gramophone" is a:

    A. record player
    B. CD player
    C. telephone
    D. computer

"The National Academy, *often* called the Recording Academy, started in 1957."

2. The word "often" best means:

    A. never
    B. only
    C. frequently
    D. always

"It wanted to put the names of *entertainers* in stars in the sidewalk."

3. The word "entertainers" means:

    A. performers
    B. lawyers
    C. songwriters
    D. conductors

"The Recording Academy received some *criticism* that first year."

4. The word "criticism" means:

    A. loyalty
    B. underestimation
    C. appreciation
    D. disapproval

"The Academy response is that the Grammys reward artistic *excellence*, not popularity."

5. The word "excellence" best means:

    A. entertaining
    B. top quality of production
    C. biggest seller
    D. better than before

"Members can make nominations in four general *categories*..."

6. The word "categories" means

    A. music
    B. group or type
    C. performer
    D. rap

WORD CHOICE

Directions: As you read this piece, you will find blanks for missing words. Three words are listed after the blank. One of these is correct. <u>Read the rest of the sentence past the blank to figure out which is the correct word</u>. Write it in the blank.

Every year the National Academy of Recording Arts and Sciences honors people in the _____ (music, arts, science) industry. Winners receive a statuette of an old-fashioned _____ (telephone, CD, record player), which was called a gramophone. The award's name is the Grammy, and is on _____ (its, it's it is) second fifty year run.

The National Academy, often _____ (calling, called, caller) the Recording Academy, started almost by accident. In 1957 the _____ (place, city, state) of Hollywood was creating a walk of _____ (pedestrians, lame, fame) on Hollywood Boulevard. It wanted to put the _____ (names, works, albums) of entertainers in stars in the sidewalk. It asked five executives of recording _____ (companies, markets, places) to suggest names. When they met, they also came up with the idea of an _____ (school, university, academy) for the music industry.

"The Grammy Awards"

LOOK WHO'S TALKING

Directions: Below are references from "The Grammy Awards." Number each paragraph. Look back in the article and re-read the paragraph in which you find the reference. Circle what you think is the best answer to each question.

1. **In the second paragraph, the first "it" best refers to:**

   A. the city
   B. the names
   C. the Academy
   D. the group of entertainers

2. **In paragraph three, the word "its" refers to:**

   A. the Academy
   B. the city
   C. the company
   D. the businesses

3. **In paragraph six, the word "he" refers to:**

   A. Elvis Presley
   B. Bobby Darin
   C. Frank Sinatra
   D. None of the above

4. **In paragraph eight the word "them" refers to:**

   A. the names
   B. the statuettes
   C. the results
   D. the companies

5. **In paragraph nine, the word "it" refers to:**

   A. the Hall of Fame
   B. the Academy
   C. the awards
   D. the contest

6. **In paragraph ten the word "they" refers to:**

   A. a billion people
   B. the artists
   C. the record companies
   D. the records

NOTE MAKING

Directions: Read the key words on the left side of the chart below. Then add notes that answer the question in parentheses under the key word.

National Academy of Recording Arts and Sciences (What?)	
Criticism (When?)	
Nominations (Why?)	
Grammy Hall of Fame (Who?)	
Walk of Fame (Where?)	

"The Grammy Awards"

IS THAT A FACT?

Directions: Read the definitions of a <u>fact</u> and an <u>inference</u> below. Then read the paragraph that follows. At the bottom of the page, write an "F" on the blank if a sentence is a fact or an "I" if it is an inference. Use the following definitions:

<u>Fact</u> – a statement that can be proven to be true from the article.

<u>Inference</u> – a guess as to what MIGHT be true.

> "The Academy's response to criticism always has remained the same. The Recording Academy insists that every year the Grammys reward artistic excellence, not popularity. In that first year, for example, the wildly popular Frank Sinatra received twelve nominations. He won only one Grammy, though, and even that was only for "Best Album Cover." Over fifty years plenty of other popular artists have failed to win at all."

_____ **1.** The Academy only rewards artistic excellence, not popularity.

_____ **2.** Frank Sinatra must have been a great singer because he was so popular.

_____ **3.** To receive a Grammy is a great honor.

_____ **4.** It is difficult to win a Grammy.

_____ **5.** Just because an artist is popular does not guarantee that he or she will win a Grammy.

_____ **6.** Many popular artists have not received Grammys.

MAKE A SPACE

Directions: Below are sentences that are missing punctuation and capitalization. First, draw slash marks (/) between the words. Then rewrite each sentence in the space below it, filling in the missing punctuation and capitalization.

Example:

The/recording/academy/received/some/criticism/that/first/year

The Recording Academy received some criticism that first year.

1. theyfoundedtherecordingacademythatsameyear

_____

2. itsmissionistorecognizemusicalexcellenceandhelpmusicmakers

_____

_____

3. itsmembersrepresentboththecreativeandthebusinesssides

_____

_____

4. winnersreceivedastatueofanoldrecordplayercalledagramophone

_____

_____

TIME MY READ # 2

Directions: With a partner, you will see how many words you can read correctly in 45 seconds. As you read, your partner will put an "X" through any word read incorrectly. Then your partner will read while you keep score. When you have both read, trade your books or papers. Count the total number of words you read correctly. Write this score at the bottom of your page.

WORD COUNT

national industry statuette honor record player gramophone Grammy anniversary	8
academy recognize entertainers companies fame excellence broadcast finalists	16
legendary business agent award ceremony broadcast jazz rhythm & blues	24
national industry statuette honor record player gramophone Grammy anniversary	32
academy recognize entertainers companies fame excellence broadcast finalists	40
legendary business agent award ceremony broadcast jazz rhythm & blues	48
national industry statuette honor record player gramophone Grammy anniversary	56
academy recognize entertainers companies fame excellence broadcast finalists	64
legendary business agent award ceremony broadcast jazz rhythm & blues	72
national industry statuette honor record player gramophone Grammy anniversary	80

Number of words read correctly _____. Is the score higher

than it was in Time My Read #1?_____

WORD PARTS

Directions: The Greek root "tele" means *far*. Draw pictures of the following words containing the root "tele."

1. television – (noun) an electrical device that receives images and sounds from far away and then sends them out.

2. telecast – (noun) a program broadcast, or played, on television.

3. telephone – (noun) an object that allows someone to hear people from far away.

4. telescope – (noun) an object used to see things that are very far away, such as objects in outer space.

television	telecast	telephone	telescope

Directions: The Greek roots "graph" and "gram" mean *write* or *describe*. Each of the following words has one of these roots in it: photograph, gramophone, graph, and biography. Write the word on the blank that describes each picture. Write 3 more words with these roots on the back.

  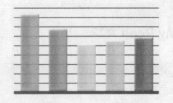 

_____ _____ _____ _____

"The Grammy Awards"

THE GRAMMY AWARDS WORD PUZZLE

Directions: Complete the crossword puzzle.

Across

1 the very best; top quality

3 a program broadcast or sent out on television

5 an old record player

10 performer

Down

2 things of a similar type: a group

4 an object used to hear people from far away

6 frequently

7 a written piece describing someone's life

8 disapproval

9 a chart that shows information about something

Word List

CATEGORY	CRITICISM	GRAMOPHONE	EXCELLENCE	OFTEN
BIOGRAPHY	ENTERTAINER	TELEPHONE	TELECAST	GRAPH

WRITING FRAME

Directions: Below is a writing frame. Use your knowledge and information from the article to complete the frame below.

Every year the National Academy of Recording Arts and Sciences honors people in the music industry. Winners receive a statuette of an old-fashioned _____, which was called a _____. The award's name is the _____.

The National Academy, often called the Recording Academy, started almost by accident. In 1957, the city of Hollywood was creating a _____. It asked five executives of recording companies to suggest names. When they met, the also got the idea of an _____.

They founded the Recording Academy that same year. Its mission is to recognize _____ and help

_____. Its members represent both the creative side of the industry, such as _____, and _____, and the business side, such as _____

_____, _____, and _____. More than a _____ from _____

_____ watch the telecast of the Grammy Awards.

"The Grammy Awards"

TAKE A STAND

Directions: People often have different feelings, or opinions, about the same thing. A "debate" is when people argue their different ideas. A good, persuasive argument has the following:

Facts – statements that can be proven to be true.

Statistics – research from a scientific study that uses numbers.

Examples – stories from the world that support an opinion.

You and a partner are going to debate two of your other classmates. The topic you are going to debate is the following:

The public really decides who wins a Grammy Award.

Decide whether you agree or disagree with this statement.
Then answer these questions in order to win your debate.

1. What are your 2 strongest points to persuade the other side?
(You can do Internet research to include facts, statistics, and examples.)

A. _____

B. _____

2. What will the other side say to argue against point A?

_____

3. What will the other side say to argue against point B?

_____

_____

4. What will you say to prove the other side's arguments are wrong?

_____

_____

Name _____ Date _____

ASSESSMENT

Comprehension: Answer the questions about the passage below.

"The National Academy, often called the Recording Academy, started almost by accident. In 1957 the city of Hollywood was creating a "Walk of Fame" on Hollywood Boulevard. It wanted to put the names of entertainers in stars in the sidewalk. It asked five executives of recording companies to suggest names. When they met, they also came up with the idea of an academy for the music industry.

They founded the Recording Academy that same year. Its mission is to recognize musical excellence, help music makers, and ensure that music remains a key part of American culture. Its members represent both the creative side of the industry (musicians, song writers, and music producers) and the business side (company executives, disc jockeys, and business agents)."

1. Who are the people involved with the Grammy Awards?

_____

_____

2. What was the author's purpose for writing about the Grammys?

_____

_____

Fluency: The words in the two sentences are all connected. The sentences are also missing punctuation and capitalization. Draw slash marks (/) between the words. Then rewrite the sentence, filling in the punctuation and capitalization.

1. in1957thecityofhollywoodwascreatingawalkoffameinhollywood

_____

_____

ASSESSMENT

2. thenationalacademyoftencalledtherecordingacademystartedbyaccident

_____

_____

Fluency: Read the three sentences below. Imagine where you would pause within each sentence as you read it aloud. Draw a slash (/) mark between the phrases where you would pause. The first slash is done.

3. It asked / five executives of recording companies to suggest names.

4. Winners receive a statuette of an old-fashioned record player that was called a gramophone.

5. Every year the National Academy of Recording Arts and Sciences honors people in the music industry.

Vocabulary: Based on what you have learned in this lesson, match the following words with their definitions. Write the letter of the definition on the blank in front of the word it defines.

1. _____ telephone	**A.** a written piece describing someone's life
2. _____ often	**B.** the very best; top quality
3. _____ biography	**C.** a performer
4. _____ criticism	**D.** an old record player
5. _____ entertainer	**E.** things of a similar type; a group
6. _____ television	**F.** disapproval
7. _____ category	**G.** a device that sends and receives images
8. _____ graph	**H.** frequently
9. _____ excellence	**I.** a device to hear people from far away
10. _____ gramophone	**J.** a chart showing information

Name _____ Date _____

ANTICIPATION GUIDE

Directions: <u>Before</u> you read the article "The Courts Rule on the Second Amendment," read the statements below. If you agree with a statement, put a check on the line. Otherwise, leave it blank.

_____ **1.** Handguns cause a huge amount of crime in cities.

_____ **2.** People need guns to protect their country.

_____ **3.** Every adult American should be allowed to own a handgun.

Once you have checked the statements above, tell why you agreed or disagreed with each statement in the section below.

1. _____

_____

2. _____

_____

3. _____

_____

In the box below, draw a picture of what you think this article is about.

What's Happening
IN THE USA?

By Lawrence Gable
© *2010 What's Happening Publications*

Subject: Human Rights

The Courts Rule on the Second Amendment

The Second Amendment to the Constitution guarantees the right to bear arms. However, it never has been clear what the amendment actually means. In March 2008 the U.S. Supreme Court heard its first case about the Second Amendment since 1939.

The Second Amendment has only 27 words. It reads:"A well regulated Militia, being necessary to the security of a free State, the right of the people to keep and bear Arms, shall not be infringed." Some people say it gives individuals the right to own firearms. Others say it gives a collective right for states to arm citizens and form militias like the National Guard.

In the case from 1939 the Court ruled that sawed-off shotguns were illegal. It said that the Second Amendment does not guarantee the right to keep such weapons, because militias do not use them. The Court did not discuss individual rights.

Nine federal appeals courts also made rulings after that. Each time they supported a collective right to bear arms, not an individual right. However, in 2007 a court ruled in favor of an individual's right to keep a handgun.

That case involved a security guard in Washington, D.C. He carried a handgun at work, and he wanted to have it at home too. The city refused his request, so he took his case to a federal court. It ruled that D.C.'s law on handguns violates the Second Amendment.

Washington, D.C., passed its law in 1976. Because of the high numbers of crimes, it required handgun owners to register them with the city. It also stopped registering any more handguns. The law did allow individuals to keep rifles and shotguns either under a trigger lock or disassembled.

The District of Columbia appealed the federal court's 2007 decision. That sent the case called *District of Columbia v. Heller* before the Supreme Court. Lawyers for Mr. Heller argued that the Second Amendment allows individuals to protect themselves in their own homes.

Lawyers for the District of Columbia argued that the amendment refers to the security of a state. In their view, the amendment gives states the right to form militias for the defense of the state. The state may arm its citizens, but there is no right for individuals to keep arms.

Others also expressed their opinions to the Supreme Court. Eleven cities argued that large cities suffer more violence from firearms than other places do, so they should be able to place reasonable restrictions on weapons. Hundreds of members of Congress asked the Court to allow citizens to keep handguns in their homes for self-defense.

Most of the debate about bearing arms centers around handguns. Cities argue that criminals can hide them too easily. If they take them onto buses and into schools and offices at work, public safety is at risk. People like Mr. Heller argued that handguns are handy, so individuals can defend themselves easily at home. Both sides accepted the need for governments to regulate military-style firearms.

In June 2008 the Supreme Court ruled 5–4 in favor of Mr. Heller. It found D.C.'s law unconstitutional, but that did not end the debate. The District of Columbia is neither a state nor a city. Therefore, it is unclear whether the ruling applies to the fifty states and cities around the U.S. In the future their public safety laws about guns might also end up before the Supreme Court.

REACTION GUIDE

Directions: <u>Now that you have read</u> "The Courts Rule on the Second Amendment," reread the statements below. Then think about how the author would feel about these statements. If you think the author would agree, put a check on the line before the number. Then, below the statement, copy the words, phrases, or sentences in the article that tell you the author's real views.

_____ **1.** Handguns cause a huge amount of crime in cities.

Article notes: _____

_____

_____ **2.** People need guns to protect their country.

Article notes: _____

_____

_____ **3.** Every adult American should be allowed to own a handgun.

Article notes: _____

_____

Name _____ Date _____

Directions: The article you are going to read is about "banning handguns." See how many boxes you can fill in below with words about the debate over handgun ownership. For example, put the word "law" in the J–L box. Try to put at least one word in every box.

A–C	D–F	G–I
J–L	**M–O**	**P–R**
S–T	**U–V**	**W–Z**

TIME MY READ # 1

Directions: With a partner, you will see how many words you can read correctly in 45 seconds. As you read, your partner will put an "X" through any word read incorrectly. Then your partner will read while you keep score. When you have both read, trade your books or papers. Count the total number of words you read correctly. Write this score at the bottom of your page.

WORD COUNT

amendment supreme regulated firearms actually militias guarantee security	8
individuals citizen registered illegal rulings ensure interference handgun	16
restrictions experts debate specify permits dispute unconstitutional arms	24
amendment supreme regulated firearms actually militias guarantee security	32
individuals citizen registered illegal rulings ensure interference handgun	40
restrictions experts debate specify permits dispute unconstitutional arms	48
amendment supreme regulated firearms actually militias guarantee security	56
individuals citizen registered illegal rulings ensure interference handgun	64
restrictions experts debate specify permits dispute unconstitutional arms	72
amendment supreme regulated firearms actually militias guarantee security	80

Number of words read correctly _____.

ECHO READING

Directions: When you read, you should make breaks between groups of words. As the teacher reads each phrase, repeat aloud what was read and underline that phrase. Then you will read the whole sentence aloud together. The first sentence has been underlined for you.

The Second Amendment to the Constitution guarantees the right to bear arms. However, it has never been clear what the amendment actually means. In March 2008 the U. S. Supreme Court heard a case about the Second Amendment for the first time since 1939.

The case from 1939 was called *United States v. Miller*. In it the court ruled that sawed-off shotguns were illegal because they played no role in maintaining a militia. It ruled that the Second Amendment does not guarantee the right to keep such a weapon, but it did not discuss individual versus collective rights.

Others also expressed their opinions about the case. In January, eleven cities sent a document to the Supreme Court. They argued that large cities suffer more violence from firearms than other places do, and that they should be able to place reasonable restrictions on weapons.

GET A CONTEXT CLUE

Directions: Below are sentences from "The Courts Rule on the Second Amendment."
Read the sentence. Look back in the article and read the paragraph the sentence is in.
Circle what you think is the best answer to each question.

"The Second Amendment to the
Constitution guarantees the right
to *bear* arms."

1. The word "bear" means:

    A.   a large furry animal
    B.   naked
    C.   own or have
    D.   steal

"Nine federal appeals *courts* also made
rulings after that."

2. The word "courts" refers to:

    A.   kings and queens
    B.   countries
    C.   the ruler or king
    D.   where judges decide conflicts

"Each time they supported a *collective*
right to bear arms, not an individual
right."

3. The word "collective" means:

    A.   a right for one person
    B.   a right to hold in your arms
    C.   a right for a group of people
    D.   a right to share weapons

"It ruled that D.C.'s law on handguns
violates the Second Amendment."

4. The word "violates" means:

    A.   breaks the rules or laws
    B.   clears up
    C.   supports
    D.   includes

"It also stopped *registering* them with
the city."

5. The word "registering" means:

    A.   allowing
    B.   signing up or documenting
    C.   fining
    D.   using or practicing

"Most of the *debate* about bearing arms
centers around handguns."

6. The word "debate" means:

    A.   trial before a judge
    B.   law
    C.   belief about something
    D.   argument between two sides

Name _____ Date _____

WORD MAP

Directions: Follow the directions to map the word in the box below.

> **restriction**

List 2 more words that mean the same.

List 2 more examples of restrictions.

List 2 opposites or non-examples.

ban

Cell phones in the classroom

allow

Draw a picture below to help you remember the meaning.

Write a definition IN YOUR OWN WORDS.

LOOK WHO'S TALKING

Directions: Below are references from "The Courts Rule on the Second Amendment." Number each paragraph. Look back in the article and re-read the paragraph in which you find the reference. Circle what you think is the best answer to each question.

1. In the second paragraph, the phrase "Others say it gives a collective right," the word "it" refers to:

   A. the amendment
   B. the Supreme Court
   C. the Constitution
   D. the law

2. In paragraph three, the word "It" refers to:

   A. the Second Amendment
   B. the Supreme Court
   C. the militias
   D. the individual's rights

3. In paragraph five, the word "it" refers to:

   A. the federal court
   B. the city
   C. the amendment
   D. the police

4. In paragraph eight, the word "their" refers to:

   A. the lawyers
   B. the state
   C. the citizens
   D. the city

5. In paragraph nine the word "they" refers to:

   A. the lawyers
   B. the cities
   C. the Congress
   D. the Supreme Court

6. In paragraph ten, the word "them" refers to:

   A. the government
   B. the city
   C. the handguns
   D. the citizens

HOW'S IT ORGANIZED?

This article is organized in **chronological order**, *or in the time order that things happened.*

Directions: Answer these questions in the spaces at the bottom.

1. When was the first case about the Second Amendment?

2. What does the Second Amendment say?

3. What was the ruling, or decision, of the 1939 Court case?

4. Since 1939, how have nine federal appeals courts ruled?

5. How did a court rule differently in 2007?

6. What was the law passed in D.C. in 1976 that the federal court decided against in 2007?

7. Where did the case go when D.C. appealed the decision?

8. What did the Supreme Court decide?

Answers:

1.	
2.	
3.	
4.	
5.	
6.	
7.	
8.	

IS THAT A FACT?

Directions: Read the definitions of a <u>fact</u> and an <u>inference</u> below. Then read the paragraph that follows. At the bottom of the page, write an "F" on the blank if a sentence is a fact or an "I" if it is an inference. Use the following definitions:

<u>Fact</u> – a statement that can be proven to be true from the article.

<u>Inference</u> – a guess as to what MIGHT be true.

"Most of the debate about bearing arms centers around handguns. Cities argue that criminals can hide them too easily. If they take them into schools, buses, or offices at work, public safety is at risk. People like Mr. Heller argued that handguns are handy so individuals can easily defend themselves at home. Both sides accepted the need for government to regulate military-style firearms. "

_____ **1.** Handguns are the major issue with this amendment.

_____ **2.** You are likely to experience a crime involving a handgun.

_____ **3.** Registering handguns is a matter of public safety.

_____ **4.** Many people enjoy owning a handgun.

_____ **5.** People agree that military-style guns need to be regulated.

_____ **6.** The Second Amendment is about a safety issue.

MAKE A SPACE

Directions: Below are sentences that are missing punctuation and capitalization. First, draw slash marks (/) between the words. Then rewrite each sentence in the space below it, filling in the missing punctuation and capitalization.

Example:

However/it/has/never/been/clear/what/the/amendment/means

However, it has never been clear what the amendment means.

1. overtheyearsninefederalappealscourtsalsohavemaderulings

_____

2. thecourtrefusedhisrequestsohiscasewenttotrial

_____

_____

3. injanuaryelevencitiessentadocumenttothesupremecourt

_____

_____

4. citiesarguethatcriminalscanhidethemtooeasily

_____

_____

TIME MY READ # 2

Directions: With a partner, you will see how many words you can read correctly in 45 seconds. As you read, your partner will put an "X" through any word read incorrectly. Then your partner will read while you keep score. When you have both read, trade your books or papers. Count the total number of words you read correctly. Write this score at the bottom of your page.

WORD COUNT

amendment supreme regulated firearms actually militias guarantee security	8
individuals citizen registered illegal rulings ensure interference handgun	16
restrictions experts debate specify permits dispute unconstitutional arms	24
amendment supreme regulated firearms actually militias guarantee security	32
individuals citizen registered illegal rulings ensure interference handgun	40
restrictions experts debate specify permits dispute unconstitutional arms	48
amendment supreme regulated firearms actually militias guarantee security	56
individuals citizen registered illegal rulings ensure interference handgun	64
restrictions experts debate specify permits dispute unconstitutional arms	72
amendment supreme regulated firearms actually militias guarantee security	80

Number of words read correctly _____. Is the score higher

than it was in Time My Read #1?_____

WORD PARTS

Directions: A **base word** is a word that can stand alone. A **prefix** is a word part added to the beginning of a base word. For example, in the word **improper**, **proper** is the base word and **im-** is the prefix added at the beginning. The prefixes **im**, **ir**, **il**, and **in** all mean "not." *Improper* means "not proper or not correct." Write a definition for the words below on the line. Do <u>not</u> use the base word in the definition. If you don't know the base word, such as *proper* in "improper," look it up in a dictionary or ask a partner.

1. illegal – _____

2. impossible – _____

3. irregular – _____

4. inaccurate – _____

5. immature – _____

6. irresponsible – _____

7. inadequate – _____

8. illogical – _____

9. immeasurable – _____

10. incorrect – _____

11. illiterate – _____

12. indefensible – _____

13. impartial – _____

14. irrational – _____

15. inexpensive – _____

SUMMARIZING ABC's

Directions: Now that you've read the article on the debate over handguns, see how many words you can fill in the boxes below.

A–C	D–F	G–I
J–L	**M–O**	**P–R**
S–T	**U–V**	**W–Z**

"The Courts Rule on the Second Amendment"

Name _____ Date _____

SENTENCE SUMMARIES

Directions: Below are 4 key words from the article "The Courts Rule on the Second Amendment." Your job is to summarize, or restate, what you've learned in this article by using these 4 words or phrases in two sentences. Then, as a challenge, try to use all 4 words or phrases in one sentence to restate the article.

FOUR KEY WORDS OR PHRASES

court(s)   Second Amendment

handgun(s)   Washington, D.C.

Sentence Summaries:

1._____

_____

2._____

_____

Challenge Summary – (All 4 words or phrases in one sentence!)

1._____

_____

_____

TAKE A STAND

Directions: People often have different feelings, or opinions, about the same thing. A "debate" is when people argue their different ideas. A good, persuasive argument has the following:

Facts – statements that can be proven to be true.

Statistics – research from a scientific study that uses numbers.

Examples – stories from the world that support an opinion.

You and a partner are going to debate two of your other classmates. The topic you are going to debate is the following:

Every adult American should be allowed to own a handgun.

Decide whether you agree or disagree with this statement.
Then answer these questions in order to win your debate.

1. What are your 2 strongest points to persuade the other side?
(You can do Internet research to include facts, statistics, and examples.)

A. _____

B. _____

2. What will the other side say to argue against point A?

_____

_____

3. What will the other side say to argue against point B?

_____

_____

4. What will you say to prove the other side's arguments are wrong?

_____

_____

Name _____ Date _____

ASSESSMENT

Comprehension: Answer the questions about the passage below.

The Second Amendment to the constitution guarantees the right to bear arms. However, it has never been clear what the amendment actually means. In March the U. S. Supreme Court heard a case about the Second Amendment for the first time since 1939. The case from 1939 was called *United States v. Miller*. It ruled that the Second Amendment does not guarantee the right to keep such a weapon, but it did not discuss individual versus collective rights.

1. What is the difference between "individual" and "collective" rights?

_____

_____

2. Why do many people think the Second Amendment allows handguns?

_____

_____

3. What was the author's purpose for writing about the Second Amendment?

_____

_____

Fluency: The words in the two sentences are all connected. The sentences are also missing punctuation and capitalization. Draw slash marks (/) between the words. Then rewrite the sentence, filling in the punctuation and capitalization.

1. ithasneverbeenclearwhatthesecondamendmentmeans

_____

_____

ASSESSMENT

2. thesecondamendmentdidnotdiscussindividualversuscollectiverights

_____

_____

Fluency: Read the three sentences below. Imagine where you would pause within each sentence as you read it aloud. Draw a slash (/) mark between the phrases where you would pause. The first slash is done.

3. Over the years / nine federal appeals courts also have made rulings.

4. In March 2008 the U. S. Supreme Court heard a case about the Second Amendment for the first time since 1939.

5. As a matter of public safety, it passed a law that required handgun owners to register them with the city.

Vocabulary: Based on what you have learned in this lesson, match the following words with their definitions. Write the letter of the definition on the blank in front of the word it defines.

1. _____ bear   **A.** not enough

2. _____ immature   **B.** cheap

3. _____ collective   **C.** an argument between two sides

4. _____ inadequate   **D.** to break the rules or laws

5. _____ illiterate   **E.** childish, not grown up

6. _____ debate   **F.** where judges and juries decide conflicts

7. _____ inexpensive   **G.** not done correctly; not normal

8. _____ violate   **H.** to hold or have, to possess

9. _____ court   **I.** a group of people

10. _____ irregular   **J.** unable to read

Name _____ Date _____

ANTICIPATION GUIDE

Directions: <u>Before</u> you read the article "Global Zero Launches Its Campaign," read the statements below. If you agree with a statement, put a check on the line. Otherwise, leave it blank.

_____ **1.** We don't have to worry about countries using nuclear weapons.

_____ **2.** We should stop countries from creating nuclear weapons.

_____ **3.** Nuclear weapons should have never been invented.

Once you have checked the statements above, tell why you agreed or disagreed with each statement in the section below.

1. _____
_____

2. _____
_____

3. _____
_____

In the box below, draw a picture of what you think this article is about.

What's Happening
IN THE WORLD?

By Lawrence Gable
© 2010 What's Happening Publications

Subject: Global Issues

Global Zero Launches Its Campaign

Humans developed nuclear weapons more than 60 years ago. The United States dropped two nuclear bombs on Japan at the end of World War II, and the world has lived in fear of them ever since. In December 2008 a new campaign to eliminate nuclear weapons began in Paris. It calls itself Global Zero.

The U.S., the United Kingdom and Canada developed the first nuclear bombs. After seven years they had made the world's most destructive weapon. The two bombs that fell on Japan in 1945 killed or injured more than 200,000 people. Those are the only two times that any country has used nuclear weapons.

Now other countries have nuclear weapons too. China, Russia, France and Britain got them after the U.S. In 1970 those five nations agreed not to spread the technology to other countries. However, India and Pakistan have developed weapons, and Israel almost certainly has several hundred. North Korea and Iran may be developing them too.

There are 27,000 nuclear weapons worldwide. The U.S. and Russia own 96 percent of them. However, people fear that unstable small countries and terrorist groups could get them too. That is why there is such interest in eliminating nuclear weapons.

It took 18 months to establish Global Zero. Finally more than 100 people met in Paris in December 2008. Among them were scientists, winners of the Nobel Peace Prize, and former and current world leaders.

Those people in Paris wrote and signed a simple declaration. Its opening line states: "We believe that to protect our children, our grandchildren and our civilization from the threat of nuclear catastrophe, we must eliminate all nuclear weapons globally."

Global Zero also launched a global public campaign. At its Web site individuals can sign that same declaration. Many thousands of people from all over the world have signed it. They also have organized local campaigns and groups on Internet sites like Facebook.

The U.S. and Russia are important to the campaign. Former President Carter and the former Soviet leader Mikhail Gorbachev have signed the declaration. In addition, Russia's Prime Minister Vladimir Putin and Barack Obama have called for the elimination of all nuclear weapons. Global Zero sent delegations to meet with leaders in Moscow and Washington, D.C.

Global Zero has outlined three steps. First, it wants Russia and the U.S. to cut the number of weapons they have. Second, it wants the other countries to join Russia and the U.S. in slowly reducing their weapons to zero. Third, it wants a system for managing nuclear fuel from power plants and preventing the development of nuclear weapons. Reaching zero could take until 2035.

Getting to zero weapons is only part of the solution. The other part is staying at zero. Countries will have to believe that no country could develop a new program or restart an old one. Beyond that, there must be a plan for responding to a crisis.

Nations agree that the dangers have increased. Eliminating nuclear weapons used to be a wild dream, but now it could happen. Global Zero held an international conference in 2010 for 500 leaders.

The campaign hopes to convince people that living with nuclear weapons is simply no way to live.

REACTION GUIDE

Directions: <u>Now that you have read</u> "Global Zero Launches Its Campaign," reread the statements below. Then think about how the author would feel about these statements. If you think the author would agree, put a check on the line before the number. Then, below the statement, copy the words, phrases, or sentences in the article that tell you the author's real views.

_____ **1.** We don't have to worry about countries using nuclear weapons.

Article notes: _____

_____

_____

_____ **2.** We should stop countries from creating nuclear weapons.

Article notes: _____

_____

_____

_____ **3.** Nuclear weapons should have never been invented.

Article notes: _____

_____

_____

WORDSTORM

Directions: It's good to know more than just the dictionary definition of a word. A wordstorm lets you write down information that helps you understand what a word means, how it's related to other words, and how to use it in different ways.

What is the word?

campaign
_____

Copy the sentence from the text in which the word is used:

_____

_____

What are some other words or phrases that mean the same thing?

_____

What are three things that happen during a campaign?

1. _____ 2. _____ 3. _____

Name three people who would likely use this word other than teachers.

1. _____ 2. _____ 3. _____

Draw a picture that reminds you of the word "campaign" below:

"Global Zero Launches Its Campaign"

Name _____ Date _____

TIME MY READ # 1

Directions: With a partner, you will see how many words you can read correctly in 45 seconds. As you read, your partner will put an "X" through any word read incorrectly. Then your partner will read while you keep score. When you have both read, trade your books or papers. Count the total number of words you read correctly. Write this score at the bottom of your page.

WORD COUNT

nuclear catastrophe campaign destructive worldwide terrorists scientists technology	8
launching declaration reducing crisis solution inspections globally unstable	16
international program responding nations eliminating dream Nobel system	24
nuclear catastrophe campaign destructive worldwide terrorists scientists technology	32
launching declaration reducing crisis solution inspections globally unstable	40
international program responding nations eliminating dream Nobel system	48
nuclear catastrophe campaign destructive worldwide terrorists scientists technology	56
launching declaration reducing crisis solution inspections globally unstable	64
international program responding nations eliminating dream Nobel system	72
nuclear catastrophe campaign destructive worldwide terrorists scientists technology	80

Number of words read correctly _____.

ECHO READING

Directions: When you read, you should make breaks between groups of words. As the teacher reads each phrase, repeat aloud what was read and underline that phrase. Then you will read the whole sentence aloud together. The first sentence has been underlined for you.

There are 27,000 nuclear weapons world-wide. The U.S. and Russia own 96 percent of them. However, people fear that unstable small countries and terrorist groups could get them too. That is why there is such interest now in eliminating nuclear weapons. It took 18 months to establish Global Zero.

Finally more than 100 people met in Paris in December. Among them were scientists, winners of the Nobel Peace Prize, and former and current world leaders. Those people in Paris wrote and signed a simple declaration. Its opening line states: "We believe that to protect our children, our grandchildren and our civilization from the threat of nuclear catastrophe, we must eliminate all nuclear weapons globally." They worry that countries could develop a new program or restart an old one.

Beyond that, there must be a plan for responding to a crisis. Nations agree that the dangers have increased. The campaign hopes to convince people that living with nuclear weapons is simply no way to live.

GET A CONTEXT CLUE

Directions: Below are sentences from "Global Zero Launches Its Campaign." Read the sentence. Look back in the article and read the paragraph the sentence is in. Then circle what you think is the best answer to each question.

"In December 2008 a new *campaign* to eliminate nuclear weapons began in Paris."

1. The word "campaign" means:

    A. charge
    B. movement
    C. idea
    D. politics

"It took 18 months to *establish* Global Zero."

2. The word "establish" means:

    A. get rid of
    B. create
    C. discuss
    D. clean up

"Those people in Paris wrote and signed a simple *declaration*."

3. The word "declaration" is:

    A. a signed statement
    B. a law
    C. a speech
    D. a vote

"*Global* Zero also launched a global public campaign."

4. The word "global" has to do with:

    A. the entire world
    B. something spread round
    C. newsworthy
    D. isolated

"Global Zero sent *delegations* to meet with leaders in Moscow and Washington, D.C."

5. The word "delegations" means:

    A. armies
    B. missiles
    C. representatives
    D. students

"Getting to zero weapons is only part of the *solution*."

6. The word "solution" means:

    A. the answer
    B. body of fluid
    C. organizations
    D. raising questions

WORD CHOICE

Directions: As you read this piece, you will find blanks for missing words. Three words are listed after the blank. One of these is correct. <u>Read the rest of the sentence past the blank to figure out which is the correct word</u>. Write it in the blank.

It took 18 months to establish Global Zero. Finally more than 100 people _____ (meeting, met, meet) in Paris that December. Among them _____ (is, were, was) scientists, winners of the Nobel Peace Prize, and former and current world _____ (leading, lead, leaders). They _____ (are, won't, were) instrumental in _____ (bringing, bring, brought) the others together.

Those people in Paris _____ (written, writing, wrote) and _____ (sign, signed, signing) a simple declaration. Global Zero _____ (will, be, would) also be launching a global public campaign. At its Web site individuals from all over the world _____ (can, could, can't) sign that same declaration. In fact, within a few hours thousands of people from all over the world had _____ (signed, signature, sign) it.

The U.S. and Russia _____ (is, are, aren't) critical to the campaign's success. After its launch in Paris, Global Zero _____ (sending, sent, send) delegations to meet with leaders of the other countries.

LOOK WHO'S TALKING

Directions: Below are sentences from "Global Zero Launches Its Campaign." Number each paragraph. Look back in the article and re-read the paragraph in which you find the reference. Circle what you think is the best answer to each question.

1. In the second paragraph, the word "those" best refers to:

A. the bombs
B. the two bombs
C. countries
D. the world

2. In paragraph three, the word "them" refers to:

A. the countries
B. the nuclear weapons
C. the nations
D. the bombs

3. In paragraph five, the word "them" refers to:

A. the bombs
B. the weapons
C. the people of Paris
D. the one hundred people

4. In paragraph seven, the word "it" refers to:

A. the declaration
B. the campaign
C. the Internet
D. Facebook

5. In paragraph nine the word "it" refers to:

A. the weapons
B. Global Zero
C. the system
D. the outline

6. In paragraph ten, the word "that" refers to:

A. countries developing weapons
B. stopping weapons development
C. staying at zero
D. responding to a crisis

NOTE MAKING

Directions: Read the key **bold** words on the left side of the chart below. Then add notes that answer the question in parentheses under the key word.

Global Zero

(What?)

nuclear weapons

(Where?)

Global Zero members

(Who?)

Three steps

(Which?)

Increased danger

(Why?)

IS THAT A FACT?

Directions: Read the definitions of a <u>fact</u> and an <u>inference</u> below. Then read the paragraph that follows. At the bottom of the page, write an "F" on the blank if a sentence is a fact or an "I" if it is an inference. Use the following definitions:

<u>Fact</u> – a statement that can be proven to be true from the article.

<u>Inference</u> – a guess as to what MIGHT be true.

"Global Zero is recommending three steps toward its goal. First, it wants Russia and the U.S. to make big cuts in the number of weapons they have. Second, it wants other countries with nuclear weapons to join Russia and the U.S in slowly reducing their weapons to zero. Third, it wants to establish an international system for managing nuclear fuel from power plants and preventing the development of nuclear weapons. Reaching zero could take until 2035."

_____ **1.** Global Zero does not trust countries to manage nuclear weapons on their own.

_____ **2.** Global Zero members know they have a difficult time ahead.

_____ **3.** Most countries are not eager to let go of their nuclear weapons.

_____ **4.** Russia and the U.S. have the most nuclear weapons.

_____ **5.** It is going to take many years to accomplish these goals.

MAKE A SPACE

Directions: Below are sentences that are missing punctuation and capitalization. First, draw slash marks (/) between the words. Then rewrite each sentence in the space below it, filling in the missing punctuation and capitalization.

Example:

now/a/number/of/countries/possess/nuclear/weapons

Now a number of countries possess nuclear weapons.

1. ittookeighteenmonthstoestablishglobalzero

_____

_____

2. gettingtozeroweaponsisonlypartofthesolution

_____

_____

_____

3. nationsagreedthatthedangershaveincreased

_____

_____

4. peoplefeelthatsmallunstablecountriesandterroristscouldgetthemtoo

_____

_____

TIME MY READ # 2

Directions: With a partner, you will see how many words you can read correctly in 45 seconds. As you read, your partner will put an "X" through any word read incorrectly. Then your partner will read while you keep score. When you have both read, trade your books or papers. Count the total number of words you read correctly. Write this score at the bottom of your page.

WORD COUNT

nuclear catastrophe campaign destructive worldwide terrorists scientists technology	8
launching declaration reducing crisis solution inspections globally unstable	16
international program responding nations eliminating dream Nobel system	24
nuclear catastrophe campaign destructive worldwide terrorists scientists technology	32
launching declaration reducing crisis solution inspections globally unstable	40
international program responding nations eliminating dream Nobel system	48
nuclear catastrophe campaign destructive worldwide terrorists scientists technology	56
launching declaration reducing crisis solution inspections globally unstable	64
international program responding nations eliminating dream Nobel system	72
nuclear catastrophe campaign destructive worldwide terrorists scientists technology	80

Number of words read correctly _____. Is the score higher

than it was in Time My Read #1?_____

WORD PARTS

Directions: A **base word** is a word that can stand alone. A **prefix** is a word part added to the beginning of a base word. For example, in the word **interoffice, office** is the base word and **inter-** is the prefix added at the beginning. The prefix **inter** means "among" or "between." *Interoffice* describes something sent or happening between different offices. Write a definition for the words below on the line. Try <u>not</u> to use the base word in the definition. If you don't know the base word, look it up in a dictionary or ask a partner.

1. interstate – _____

2. interplay – _____

3. international – _____

4. interracial – _____

5. interlock – _____

6. interview – _____

7. intersection – _____

8. intermingle – _____

9. intertwine – _____

10. interface – _____

11. interact – _____

12. interchange – _____

13. interstellar – _____

14. interfaith – _____

15. intercollegiate – _____

GLOBAL ZERO WORD PUZZLE

Directions: Complete the crossword puzzle.

Across

2 an answer to something

4 the entire world

7 a movement to make something happen

8 to work together

9 to ask someone about his or her life

10 between or among many countries

Down

1 a strong, signed statement

3 among different religions

5 between two or more states

6 a place where roads meet

Word List

GLOBAL	SOLUTION	INTERSECTION	CAMPAIGN	DECLARATION
INTERACT	INTERSTATE	INTERFAITH	INTERNATIONAL	INTERVIEW

WRITING FRAME

Directions: Below is a writing frame. Use your knowledge and information from the article to complete the frame below.

Humans developed nuclear weapons a little more than sixty years ago. The U.S. ended WWII by _____ _____. In December of 2008, a new campaign was launched by _____. The purpose of the campaign is to _____.

The first nuclear weapons were developed by the U.S., _____ and _____. Now a number of other countries possess them, including _____, _____, _____, _____, _____ and _____.

It took eighteen months to establish Global Zero. At the first meeting in Paris, they signed a _____ that said we must eliminate _____. Global Zero recommends these three steps toward its goal:

1. _____

2. _____

3. _____

Reaching zero could take _____.

Name _____ Date _____

TAKE A STAND

Directions: People often have different feelings, or opinions, about the same thing.
A "debate" is when people argue their different ideas. A good, persuasive argument
has the following:

Facts – statements that can be proven to be true.

Statistics – research from a scientific study that uses numbers.

Examples – stories from the world that support an opinion.

You and a partner are going to debate two of your other classmates. The topic you are going to
debate is the following:

> *We should stop countries from creating their first nuclear weapons.*

Decide whether you agree or disagree with this statement.
Then answer these questions in order to win your debate.

1. What are your 2 strongest points to persuade the other side?
   (You can do Internet research to include facts, statistics, and examples.)

A. _____

B. _____

2. What will the other side say to argue against point A?

_____

_____

3. What will the other side say to argue against point B?

_____

_____

4. What will you say to prove the other side's arguments are wrong?

_____

_____

Name _____ Date _____

ASSESSMENT

Comprehension: Answer the questions about the passage below.

It took 18 months to establish Global Zero. Finally more than 100 people met in Paris in December. The meeting included scientists, winners of the Nobel Peace Prize, and former and current world leaders. In Paris people wrote and signed a simple declaration. Global Zero is also launching a global public campaign. At its Web site individuals from all over the world can sign that same declaration. In fact, within a few hours thousands of people from 85 different countries had signed it. The campaign hopes to control nuclear weapons.

1. Why is the nuclear weapons debate so important?

_____

_____

2. What might happen if the international community doesn't control the development of nuclear weapons?

_____

_____

3. What do you think is the author's purpose in writing this article?

_____

_____

Fluency: The words in the two sentences are all connected. The sentences are also missing punctuation and capitalization. Draw slash marks (/) between the words. Then rewrite the sentence, filling in the punctuation and capitalization.

1. peoplerealizethatgettingtozeroweaponsisonlypartofthesolution

_____

_____

ASSESSMENT

2. humansdevelopednuclearweaponsoversixtyyyearsagoandnowmanycountrieshavethem

_____

_____

Fluency: Read the three sentences below. Imagine where you would pause within each sentence as you read it aloud. Draw a slash (/) mark between the phrases where you would pause. The first slash is done.

3. Getting to zero weapons / is only part of the solution.

4. Nations agree that the dangers of nuclear weapons have increased.

5. However, terrorists and small unstable countries might get them.

Vocabulary: Based on what you have learned in this lesson, match the following words with their definitions. Write the letter of the definition on the blank in front of the word it defines.

1. _____ interfaith   **A.** an answer to something

2. _____ solution   **B.** between two or more states

3. _____ declaration   **C.** a strong, signed statement

4. _____ interact   **D.** having to do with the whole world

5. _____ interview   **E.** a movement to make something happen

6. _____ campaign   **F.** among different religions

7. _____ intersection   **G.** to work together

8. _____ international   **H.** to ask someone about his or her life

9. _____ global   **I.** a place where roads meet

10. _____ interstate   **J.** between or among many nations

Name _____ Date _____

ANTICIPATION GUIDE

Directions: <u>Before</u> you read the article "The Harlem Globetrotters," read the statements below. If you agree with a statement, put a check on the line. Otherwise, leave it blank.

_____ **1.** Basketball has always been a sport for everyone.

_____ **2.** A comedy team helped start the National Basketball Association.

_____ **3.** The Harlem Globetrotters are the best thing to happen to basketball.

Once you have checked the statements above, tell why you agreed or disagreed with each statement in the section below.

1. _____

_____

2. _____

_____

3. _____

_____

In the box below, draw a picture of what you think this article is about.

By Lawrence Gable
© 2010 What's Happening Publications

Subject: Sports

The Globetrotters Still Know How to Play the Game!

In the 1920s some young Black men in Chicago formed a basketball team. When 24-year-old Abe Saperstein took control of the team, they began playing teams in small towns all around the U.S. Ever since then fans have known this team as the Harlem Globetrotters.

The team began traveling as the "New York Globetrotters." Whites in small towns were shocked when Black players arrived, because Blacks were not allowed to play pro basketball then. Adding "Harlem" to the name identified it as a Black team.

The Globetrotters played their first game in January 1927. Three hundred fans attended. The team traveled to small towns in Mr. Saperstein's car. Their first game in a major city came in Detroit in 1932.

The Globetrotters won most games easily. Then in 1939 they were leading a game 112–5, so they began to clown around. The crowd loved it, so the team started doing it regularly. It developed entertaining routines with fantastic dribbling, passing and trick shots.

The players entertained fans, but their goal still was to win games. In fact, in 1940 the Globetrotters won the World Basketball Championship. Then in 1948 and 1949 they beat the best pro team, the Minneapolis Lakers. In the "World Series of Basketball" the Globetrotters played a series of games every year against the best college players. The Globetrotters won every series from 1950 to 1958.

The Globetrotters helped the National Basketball Association (NBA) develop. After the Lakers' losses to the Globetrotters, the NBA signed its first Black players in 1950. The Globetrotters also helped attract fans to the young league by playing games before some of the NBA's games.

Because the Globetrotters were so good, many small-town teams did not want to play them. So in 1953 Mr. Saperstein convinced a friend to develop a team to oppose the Globetrotters regularly. The Washington Generals became the team's traveling opponents. They lost thousands of games to the Globetrotters.

In the 1950s the Globetrotters' fame spread. They made their first tours of other continents. At home they appeared on national television. The team developed four different squads, and each one played every night.

Basketball's Hall of Fame has honored the Globetrotters. It has inducted both Mr. Saperstein and the organization itself. Several players are also in the Hall. Marques Haynes was a magnificent dribbler and passer. Meadowlark Lemon played for 24 years and won fans with his charm and incredible hook shot from half court.

Unfortunately the team's popularity fell in the 1970s and 1980s. The tremendous growth of the NBA and college basketball took fans away. Also, several TV shows made the Globetrotters into cartoon characters. People had forgotten that the Globetrotters are fine players. In the 1990s they began scheduling tough games against college teams, and fans returned.

The Harlem Globetrotters introduced most of the world to basketball. They have played more than 22,000 games in 118 countries. Now they hope to play games every year against the NBA champion, the college champion, and international teams. After entertaining many millions of people for decades, the team still can play serious basketball.

REACTION GUIDE

Directions: Now that you have read "The Harlem Globetrotters," reread the statements below. Then think about how the author would feel about these statements. If you think the author would agree, put a check on the line before the number. Then, below the statement, copy the words, phrases, or sentences in the article that tell you the author's real views.

_____ **1.** Basketball has always been a sport for everyone.

Article notes: _____

_____

_____

_____ **2.** A comedy team helped start the National Basketball Association.

Article notes: _____

_____

_____

_____ **3.** The Harlem Globetrotters are the best thing to happen to basketball.

Article notes: _____

_____

_____

Name _____ Date _____

PREDICTING ABC's

Directions: The article you are going to read is about "basketball." See how many boxes you can fill in below with words about basketball. For example, put the word "foul" in the D–F box. Try to put at least one word in every box.

A–C	D–F	G–I
J–L	**M–O**	**P–R**
S–T	**U–V**	**W–Z**

Name _____ Date _____

TIME MY READ # 1

Directions: With a partner, you will see how many words you can read correctly in 45 seconds. As you read, your partner will put an "X" through any word read incorrectly. Then your partner will read while you keep score. When you have both read, trade your books or papers. Count the total number of words you read correctly. Write this score at the bottom of your page.

WORD COUNT

dribblers passers routine entertainment incorporate tremendous team major	8
games integrate sports crowd tough million identified basketball	16
trick shots traveled fans professionals championship Meadowlark donated	24
dribblers passers routine entertainment incorporate tremendous team major	32
games integrate sports crowd tough million identified basketball	40
trick shots traveled fans professionals championship Meadowlark donated	48
dribblers passers routine entertainment incorporate tremendous team major	56
games integrate sports crowd tough million identified basketball	64
trick shots traveled fans professionals championship Meadowlark donated	72
dribblers passers routine entertainment incorporate tremendous team major	80

Number of words read correctly _____.

ECHO READING

Directions: When you read, you should make breaks between groups of words. As the teacher reads each phrase, repeat aloud what was read and underline that phrase. Then you will read the whole sentence aloud together. The first sentence has been underlined for you.

Even though the team incorporated entertainment into its play, its goal was still to win games. In fact, in 1940 the Globetrotters won the World Basketball Championship. Then in 1948 and 1949 they beat the sport's best team, the Minneapolis Lakers. In the "World Series of Basketball" the Globetrotters played against a team of college All-Americans. The Globetrotters won every series from 1950 to 1958.

The Globetrotters helped in the development of the National Basketball Association (NBA). After the Lakers' losses to the Globetrotters the NBA signed its first Black players in 1950. The Globetrotters also helped attract fans to the young league by playing a game before the NBA's game. These were almost the only time that the young league's arenas were sold out.

In the 1950s the Globetrotters' fame spread. They made their first tour of other continents. At home they appeared on national television. The team developed four different squads, and each one played every night.

GET A CONTEXT CLUE

Directions: Below are sentences from "The Harlem Globetrotters." Read the sentence. Look back in the article and read the paragraph the sentence is in. Circle what you think is the best answer to each question.

"Adding Harlem to the name *identified* it as a Black team."

1. The word "identified" means:

    A. recognized or known
    B. an ID card
    C. isolate
    D. find

"The crowd loved it, so the team started doing it *regularly*."

2. The word "regularly" means:

    A. once in a while
    B. often or frequently
    C. as needed
    D. never ending

"It *developed* entertaining routines with fantastic dribbling, passing and trick shots."

3. The word "developed" means:

    A. created
    B. tried
    C. lacked
    D. required

"The Globetrotters also helped *attract* fans to the young league by playing games before some of the NBA's games."

4. The word "attract" means:

    A. to criticize
    B. to train
    C. to pay for
    D. to invite or draw in

"It had *inducted* both Mr. Saperstein and the organization itself."

5. The word "inducted" means:

    A. fined
    B. thought about
    C. brought in as a member
    D. placed

"Unfortunately the team's *popularity* fell in the 1970s."

6. The word "popularity" means:

    A. fame
    B. finances
    C. wins
    D. membership

Name _____ Date _____

WORD MAP

Directions: Follow the directions to map the word in the box below.

prejudice

List 2 more words
that mean the same.

List 2 more examples.

List 2 opposites
or non-examples.

hatred

Schools separated
by race

open-minded

Draw a picture below to help
you remember the meaning.

Write a definition IN
YOUR OWN WORDS.

HOW'S IT ORGANIZED?

This article is organized in **chronological order,** *or in the time order that things happened.*

Directions: Answer these questions in the spaces at the bottom.

1. When did young Black men first travel as a basketball team?

2. Why did Mr. Saperstein change the team's name in the 1920s?

3. What did the team do differently in 1939?

4. What did the Globetrotters achieve in 1948 and 1949?

5. What did the NBA do after the Globetrotters won in 1950?

6. Why did Mr. Saperstein create the Washington Generals in 1953?

7. What caused the team's popularity to fall in the 1970s and 1980s?

8. What caused fans to return in the 1990s?

Answers:

1.	
2.	
3.	
4.	
5.	
6.	
7.	
8.	

LOOK WHO'S TALKING

Directions: Below are sentences from "The Harlem Globetrotters." Number each paragraph. Look back in the article and re-read the paragraph in which you find the reference. Circle what you think is the best answer to each question.

1. In the fourth paragraph, the word "they" best refers to:

    A. the audience

    B. the towns

    C. the routines

    D. the team

2. In paragraph six, the word "its" refers to:

    A. the Globetrotters

    B. the NBA

    C. the Lakers

    D. the World Basketball Championship

3. In paragraph six, the phrase "young league" refers to:

    A. the NBA

    B. the players' ages

    C. the World Basketball Championship

    D. the owners

4. In paragraph seven, the word "they" refers to:

    A. the Generals

    B. the Globetrotters

    C. the Lakers

    D. the small-town teams

5. In paragraph eight in the last sentence, the words "each one" refers to:

    A. the Globetrotters

    B. the Generals

    C. the different squads

    D. the small-town teams

6. In paragraph ten, in the final sentence, the word "they" refers to:

    A. the league

    B. the Globetrotters

    C. the NBA

    D. the college teams

IS THAT A FACT?

Directions: Read the definitions of a <u>fact</u> and an <u>inference</u> below. Then read the paragraph that follows. At the bottom of the page, write an "F" on the blank if a sentence is a fact. Write an "I" if the sentence is an inference. Use the following definitions:

<u>Fact</u> – a statement that can be proven to be true from the article.

<u>Inference</u> – a guess as to what MIGHT be true.

> "The team began traveling as the New York Globetrotters. Whites in small towns were shocked when Black players arrived, because Blacks were not allowed to play pro basketball then. Adding the word "Harlem" identified the team as a Black team. They won their games easily, so they started to entertain the fans. The crowd loved it so the team started doing it regularly. The Globetrotters helped in the development of today's NBA. After they beat the Lakers, the NBA signed its first Black players in 1950."

_____ **1.** The Globetrotters had an important effect on how people thought of African-Americans.

_____ **2.** Basketball was once a segregated sport.

_____ **3.** The fact that it was a team with Black players was a new thing.

_____ **4.** The Globetrotters helped to integrate the NBA.

_____ **5.** Globetrotter players were some of the best in basketball.

_____ **6.** If the Globetrotters had not appeared, the NBA might not have become integrated.

"The Harlem Globetrotters"

Name _____ Date _____

MAKE A SPACE

Directions: Below are sentences that are missing punctuation and capitalization. First, draw slash marks (/) between the words. Then rewrite each sentence in the space below it, filling in the missing punctuation and capitalization.

> Example:
>
> theglobetrotterswonmostgameseasily
>
> The/Globetrotters/won/most/games/easily.

1. theplayersentertainedfansbuttheirgoalwastowingames

_____

_____

2. becausetheglobetrottersweresogoodsmalltownteamsdidnotplaythem

_____

_____

3. thetremendousgrowthofthenbaandcollegebasketballtookawayfans

_____

_____

4. theharlemglobetrottersintroducedmostoftheworldtobasketball

_____

_____

Name _____ Date _____

TIME MY READ # 2

Directions: With a partner, you will see how many words you can read correctly in 45 seconds. As you read, your partner will put an "X" through any word read incorrectly. Then your partner will read while you keep score. When you have both read, trade your books or papers. Count the total number of words you read correctly. Write this score at the bottom of your page.

WORD COUNT

dribblers passers routine entertainment incorporate tremendous team major	8
games integrate sports crowd tough million identified basketball	16
trick shots traveled fans professionals championship Meadowlark donated	24
dribblers passers routine entertainment incorporate tremendous team major	32
games integrate sports crowd tough million identified basketball	40
trick shots traveled fans professionals championship Meadowlark donated	48
dribblers passers routine entertainment incorporate tremendous team major	56
games integrate sports crowd tough million identified basketball	64
trick shots traveled fans professionals championship Meadowlark donated	72
dribblers passers routine entertainment incorporate tremendous team major	80

Number of words read correctly _____. Is the score higher

than it was in Time My Read #1?_____

WORD PARTS

Directions: A **base word** is a word that can stand alone. A **prefix** is a word part added to the beginning of a base word. For example, in the word **unequal, equal** is the base word and **un-** is the prefix added at the beginning. The prefix **un** means "not." *Unequal* means "not the same" or "not fair for all." Think of 10 words that you can add the prefix **un-** to and write them on the lines below. Share the words and their definitions with the rest of the class.

1. _____   2. _____

3. _____   4. _____

5. _____   6. _____

7. _____   8. _____

9. _____   10. _____

Directions: A **suffix** is a word part added to the end of a base word. For example, in the word *softly*, "soft" is the base word and **-ly** is the suffix added at the end. The suffix **-ly** turns the **adjective** "soft" into an **adverb,** telling how something is done. *Softly* means "done quietly or tenderly." Think of 10 words that you can add the suffix **-ly** to and write them on the lines below. Share the words and their definitions with the rest of the class.

1. _____   2. _____

3. _____   4. _____

5. _____   6. _____

7. _____   8. _____

9. _____   10. _____

SUMMARIZING ABC's

Directions: Now that you've read the article on the Harlem Globetrotters, see how many basketball words you can fill in the boxes.

A–C	D–F	G–I
J–L	M–O	P–R
S–T	U–V	W–Z

"The Harlem Globetrotters"

149

SENTENCE SUMMARIES

Directions: Below are 4 key words from the article "The Harlem Globetrotters." Your job is to summarize, or restate, what you've learned in this article by using these 4 words or phrases in two sentences. Then, as a challenge, try to use all 4 words or phrases in one sentence to restate the article.

FOUR KEY WORDS OR PHRASES

Globetrotters   college teams

National Basketball Association   black players

Sentence Summaries:

1. _____

_____

2. _____

_____

Challenge Summary (All 4 words or phrases in one sentence!)

1. _____

_____

_____

Name _____ Date _____

TAKE A STAND

Directions: People often have different feelings, or opinions, about the same thing. A "debate" is when people argue their different ideas. A good, persuasive argument has the following:

Facts – statements that can be proven to be true.

Statistics – research from a scientific study that uses numbers.

Examples – stories from the world that support an opinion.

You and a partner are going to debate two of your other classmates. The topic you are going to debate is the following:

The Harlem Globetrotters are the best thing to happen to basketball.

Decide whether you agree or disagree with this statement.
Then answer these questions in order to win your debate.

1. What are your 2 strongest points to persuade the other side?
(You can do Internet research to include facts, statistics, and examples.)

A. _____

B. _____

2. What will the other side say to argue against point A?

_____

_____

3. What will the other side say to argue against point B?

_____

_____

4. What will you say to prove the other side's arguments are wrong?

_____

_____

ASSESSMENT

Comprehension: Answer the questions about the passage below.

The Globetrotters helped the National Basketball Association (NBA) develop. After the Lakers' losses to the Globetrotters, the NBA signed its first Black players in 1950. The Globetrotters also helped attract fans to the young league by playing games before some of the NBA's games.

The Harlem Globetrotters introduced most of the world to basketball. They have played more than 22,000 games in 118 countries. They hope to play games every year against the NBA, college, and international champions.

1. What caused the NBA to start hiring Black players?

_____

_____

2. What were some of the positive things that resulted from the Globetrotters' playing basketball?

_____

_____

3. What was the author's purpose for writing about the Globetrotters?

_____

_____

Fluency: The words in the two sentences are all connected. The sentences are also missing punctuation and capitalization. Draw slash marks (/) between the words. Then rewrite the sentence, filling in the punctuation and capitalization.

1. theplayersentertainedfansbuttheirgoalwastowingames

_____

_____

ASSESSMENT

2. peoplehadforgottenthattheglobetrottersarefineplayers

_____

_____

Fluency: Read the three sentences below. Imagine where you would pause within each sentence as you read it aloud. Draw a slash (/) mark between the phrases where you would pause. The first slash is done.

3. The Globetrotters/won most games easily, so they entertained.

4. Whites in small towns were shocked to see Black players arrive, because Blacks were not allowed to play pro basketball then.

5. In the 1990s they began scheduling tough games against college teams, and now fans have returned.

Vocabulary: Based on what you have learned in this lesson, match the following words with their definitions. Write the letter of the definition on the blank in front of the word it defines.

1. _____ unpleasant   **A.** often or frequently

2. _____ identified   **B.** brought in as a member

3. _____ quickly   **C.** judgment made before knowing the facts

4. _____ uncertain   **D.** invite or draw in

5. _____ regularly   **E.** recognized or known

6. _____ prejudice   **F.** not nice

7. _____ popularity   **G.** created

8. _____ developed   **H.** fame

9. _____ attract   **I.** not sure

10. _____ inducted   **J.** fast

Name _____ Date _____

ANTICIPATION GUIDE

Directions: <u>Before</u> you read the article "Venice Puts Up a Defense," read the statements below. If you agree with a statement, put a check on the line. Otherwise, leave it blank.

_____ **1.** Too much rain always causes flooding.

_____ **2.** People can make a place worse by trying to make it better.

_____ **3.** People should stop nature from destroying old historic places.

Once you have checked the statements above, tell why you agreed or disagreed with each statement in the section below.

1. _____

_____

2. _____

_____

3. _____

_____

In the box below, draw a picture of what you think this article is about.

What's Happening
IN THE WORLD?

By Lawrence Gable
© 2010 What's Happening Publications

Subject: Environment

Venice Puts Up a Defense

Venice is one of the world's most beautiful cities. It lies in northeastern Italy on the Adriatic Sea. Its streets are canals, so people travel around in boats. Unfortunately high tides push water into Venice too often, so the city is building a barrier against the sea.

The city's 118 small islands lie in the center of a lagoon. A long sandbar divides the lagoon from the sea, but water enters the lagoon at three inlets. Every six hours the sea's tides either send some water in or pull it back out naturally.

Natural protection from the tides has almost vanished. Salt marshes once filled much of the lagoon, but most of them are gone. The government dug deep channels that replaced the gentle shallow waters. That has brought powerful water movement that erodes the marshland, islands and sandbars.

Venice has a long history of high water known as *acqua alta*. The water flows onto the city's squares and above the buildings' foundations. A century ago it happened about seven times a year. Now it happens a hundred times. People have to wear rubber boots and walk on elevated wooden boards.

The water rises high enough to damage buildings. It eats away at the brick walls above the stone foundations. That weakens them and makes them crumble. Now water seeps into homes and shops through the sewage pipes. Most Venetians no longer live on the ground floors.

Two things cause the increase in high water. One is that the city has been sinking. In the 16th century the city diverted major rivers from flowing into the lagoon. That kept silt from settling in the canals. Also, last century the city pumped fresh groundwater and gas from underground. The water table decreased and Venice's islands sank 11 inches.

The other thing is that global warming is causing the sea level to rise. Venice feels the effects of it because it lies at sea level. Experts expect a rise in the seas of at least 12 inches in this century.

A flood in November 1966 changed everything. Heavy rain and high tides pushed the water in the lagoon four feet higher than normal. Then the *sirocco* winds prevented it from flowing back out. When the next high tide came, it put Venice under six feet of water. People were trapped for three days without power or heat. Sewage and dead rats floated in the canals. That flood led to a law to save Venice.

In 2003 the government began the MOSE project. It is putting 79 hollow mobile gates at the three inlets. Normally they will lie flat on the sea floor and not affect the flow of water. However, during high waters managers will pump air into them. That will make them rise and form a barrier against the entering tide.

The gates will close when the forecast calls for a tide to rise 43 inches above normal. That will happen only about five times a year. The gates will be able to hold back seawater that is six feet higher than the level of the lagoon.

High waters in Venice have become too frequent for comfort. Many Venetians have moved away from the city, but about 20 million tourists visit Venice every year. MOSE will be finished in 2011. Then high waters and flooding may be a thing of the past for the residents and tourists in Venice, one of the world's great treasures.

REACTION GUIDE

Directions: <u>Now that you have read</u> "Venice Puts Up a Defense," reread the statements below. Then think about how the author would feel about these statements. If you think the author would agree, put a check on the line before the number. Then, below the statement, copy the words, phrases, or sentences in the article that tell you the author's real views.

_____ **1.** Too much rain always causes flooding.

Article notes: _____

_____

_____

_____ **2.** People can make a place worse by trying to make it better.

Article notes: _____

_____

_____

_____ **3.** People should stop nature from destroying old historic places.

Article notes: _____

_____

_____

WORDSTORM

Directions: It's good to know more than just the dictionary definition of a word. A wordstorm lets you write down information that helps you understand what a word means, how it's related to other words, and how to use it in different ways.

What is the word?

defense

_____

Copy the sentence from the text in which the word is used:

_____

_____

What are some other words or phrases that mean the same thing?

_____

What are three examples of how the word "defense" is used?

1. _____ 2. _____ 3. _____

Name three people who would likely use this word other than

teachers.

1. _____ 2. _____ 3. _____

Draw a picture that reminds you of the word "defense" below:

Name _____ Date _____

TIME MY READ # 1

Directions: With a partner, you will see how many words you can read correctly in 45 seconds. As you read, your partner will put an "X" through any word read incorrectly. Then your partner will read while you keep score. When you have both read, trade your books or papers. Count the total number of words you read correctly. Write this score at the bottom of your page.

WORD COUNT

global warming century lagoon sewage canals flowing elevated	8
underground sandbars sewage residents tide unfortunately tourists treasures	16
damage seawater flooding climate architecture forecast experts diverted	24
global warming century lagoon sewage canals flowing elevated	32
underground sandbars sewage residents tide unfortunately tourists treasures	40
damage seawater flooding climate architecture forecast experts diverted	48
global warming century lagoon sewage canals flowing elevatede	56
underground sandbars sewage residents tide unfortunately tourists treasures	64
damage seawater flooding climate architecture forecast experts diverted	72
global warming century lagoon sewage canals flowing elevated	80

Number of words read correctly _____.

ECHO READING

Directions: When you read, you should make breaks between groups of words. As the teacher reads each phrase, repeat aloud what was read and underline that phrase. Then you will read the whole sentence aloud together. The first sentence has been underlined for you.

Venice has a long history of high water known as "acqua alta." The water flows onto the city's squares and above the buildings' foundations. A century ago it happened about seven times a year. Now it happens a hundred times. People have to wear rubber boots and walk on elevated wooden boards.

Two things cause the increase in water. One is that the city has been sinking. In the sixteenth century the city diverted the major rivers from flowing into the lagoon. That kept the silt from settling in the canals. The second reason is that global warming is causing the sea level to rise. Venice feels the effects of global warming because it sits at sea level. Experts expect the sea to rise twelve inches a year.

GET A CONTEXT CLUE

Directions: Below are sentences from "Venice Puts Up a Defense." Read the sentence. Look back in the article and read the paragraph the sentence is in. Circle what you think is the best answer to each question.

"Unfortunately high tides push water into Venice too often, so the city is building a barrier against the sea."

1. The word "barrier" means:

    A. tower to see over something
    B. wall to block something
    C. island
    D. ship to sail away on

"Natural protection from the tides has almost vanished."

2. The word "vanished" means:

    A. grown
    B. disappeared
    C. finished
    D. opened

"Venice has a long history of high water known as *acqua alta*"

3. The phrase "*acqua alta*" means:

    A. sewage
    B. crumbling buildings
    C. canals
    D. high tides or water

"People have to wear rubber boots and walk on elevated wooden boards."

4. The word "elevated" means:

    A. lowered
    B. rotten
    C. raised or lifted up
    D. old

"In the 16th century the city diverted major rivers from flowing into the lagoon."

5. The word "diverted" means:

    A. stopped
    B. increased
    C. turned away
    D. started

"It is putting 79 hollow mobile gates at the three inlets."

6. The term "mobile" means:

    A. movable
    B. strong
    C. waterproof
    D. new

WORD CHOICE

Directions: As you read this piece, you will find blanks for missing words. Three words are listed after the blank. One of these is correct. <u>Read the rest of the sentence past the blank to figure out which is the correct word</u>. Write it in the blank.

Venice is one of the most beautiful cities in the world. It _____ (lie, lied, lies) in northeastern Italy on the Adriatic Sea. Instead of streets it _____ (had, have, has) canals, so people travel around in boats. Unfortunately, high tides _____ (pushing, pushes, push) water into Venice too often, so the city _____ (is, are, were) building a barrier against the sea.

The city's 118 small islands lie in the center of a lagoon. A long strip of sandbars _____ (divide, divided, divides) the lagoon from the sea, but water does _____ (entrance, enter, enters) the lagoon. Every six hours the Adriatic Sea's tides either rise or _____ (fell, fall, fill), sending some water into the lagoon or _____ (pulled, pulls, pulling) it back out naturally.

Natural protection from the Adriatic's tides _____ (has, have, having) almost vanished. Salt marshes once _____ (occupied, presented, stole) much of the lagoon, but most of them are gone.

LOOK WHO'S TALKING

Directions: Below are sentences from "Venice Puts Up a Defense." Number each paragraph. Look back in the article and re-read the paragraph in which you find the reference. Circle what you think is the best answer to each question.

1. **In the first paragraph, the word "its" best refers to:**

   A. the city of Venice
   B. the country of Italy
   C. the buildings
   D. the sea

2. **In paragraph two, the word "it" refers to:**

   A. the sea
   B. the tides
   C. the water
   D. the city

3. **In paragraph three, the word "that" refers to:**

   A. the response of the government
   B. the digging of the channels
   C. the pulling of the water
   D. the eroding of the marshland

4. **In paragraph seven, the phrase "The other thing" refers to:**

   A. the cause of increasing water
   B. the city sinking
   C. diverting the rivers
   D. one of the reasons the water rises

5. **In paragraph eight in the sentence "When the next high tide came, it put Venice under six feet of water," the word "it" refers to:**

   A. the tide
   B. the city
   C. global warming
   D. the flood

6. **In paragraph ten, the second sentence begins with the word "That," which refers to:**

   A. the rising tide
   B. the gates
   C. the seawater
   D. the lagoon

Name _____ Date _____

Directions: Read the key **bold** words on the left side of the chart below. Then add notes that answer the question in parentheses under the key word.

Venice

(Where?)

Acqua alta

(What?)

Flooding

(Why? Give 2 reasons)

Law to save Venice

(When?)

MOSE

(What?)

"Venice Puts Up a Defense"

IS THAT A FACT?

Directions: Read the definitions of a <u>fact</u> and an <u>inference</u> below. Then read the paragraph that follows. At the bottom of the page, write an "F" on the blank if a sentence is a fact or an "I" if it is an inference. Use the following definitions:

<u>Fact</u> – a statement that can be proven to be true from the article.

<u>Inference</u> – a guess as to what MIGHT be true.

A flood in November of 1966 changed everything. Heavy rain and high tides pushed the water in the lagoon four feet higher than normal. Then the high winds prevented it from flowing back out. When the next high tide came, it put Venice under six feet of water. People were trapped for three days without power or heat. Sewage and dead rats floated in the canals. That flood led Venice to begin the MOSE project that could save the city from flooding.

_____ **1.** Winds can affect flooding.

_____ **2.** The city of Venice is not prepared for large floods.

_____ **3.** The water level around Venice is always changing.

_____ **4.** The MOSE project is designed to combat the rising water.

_____ **5.** Venice is not a very sanitary, or clean, place.

_____ **6.** The November 1966 flood was a turning point.

TIME MY READ # 2

Directions: With a partner, you will see how many words you can read correctly in 45 seconds. As you read, your partner will put an "X" through any word read incorrectly. Then your partner will read while you keep score. When you have both read, trade your books or papers. Count the total number of words you read correctly. Write this score at the bottom of your page.

WORD COUNT

global warming century lagoon sewage canals flowing elevated	8
underground sandbars sewage residents tide unfortunately tourists treasures	16
damage seawater flooding climate architecture forecast experts diverted	24
global warming century lagoon sewage canals flowing elevated	32
underground sandbars sewage residents tide unfortunately tourists treasures	40
damage seawater flooding climate architecture forecast experts diverted	48
global warming century lagoon sewage canals flowing elevated	56
underground sandbars sewage residents tide unfortunately tourists treasures	64
damage seawater flooding climate architecture forecast experts diverted	72
global warming century lagoon sewage canals flowing elevated	80

Number of words read correctly _____. Is the score higher than it was in

Time My Read #1? _____

Name _____ Date _____

MAKE A SPACE

Directions: Below are sentences that are missing punctuation and capitalization. First, draw slash marks (/) between the words. Then rewrite each sentence in the space below it, filling in the missing punctuation and capitalization.

> Example:
>
> floodinghappensmoreoftentodaythanacenturyago
>
> Flooding/happens/more/often/today/than/a/century/ago.

1. globalwarmingiscausingthesealeveltorise

_____

_____

2. asandbardividesthelagoonfromtheseabutwatercomesinfrominlets

_____

_____

3. heavyrainsandhightidespushedwaterintothelagoon

_____

_____

4. thewatercaneatawayatbrickwallsandatthefoundationsofhomes

_____

_____

WORD PARTS

Directions: Read the definitions below. In each box on the map, write the number of the word that identifies what the box is indicating.

1. sandbar – (noun) a thin strip of land formed by the waves and currents of water.

2. lagoon – (noun) an area of shallow water separated from the sea by a sandbar or strip of land.

3. canal – (noun) a long narrow passage for water.

4. channel – (noun) a wide, deep waterway

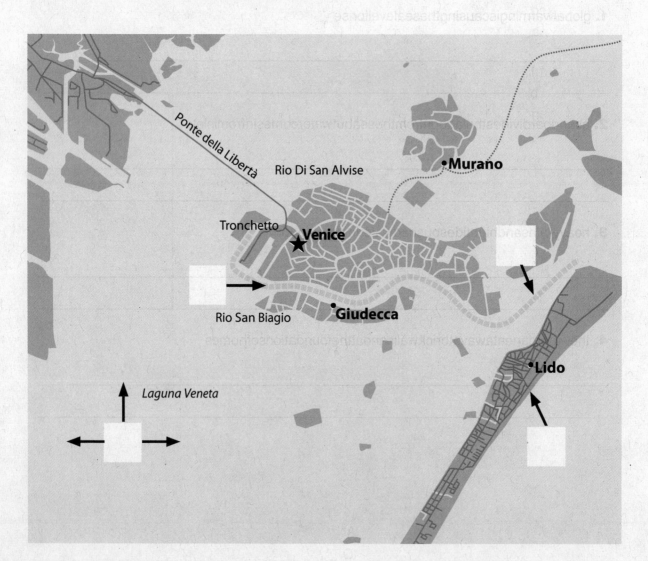

VENICE WORD PUZZLE

Directions: Complete the crossword puzzle.

Across

2 a wide, deep waterway

4 a thin strip of land formed by waves

6 turned away

7 disappeared

9 movable

Down

1 an area of shallow water separated from the sea

2 a long, narrow passage of water

3 raised or lifted up

5 a wall to block something

8 protection

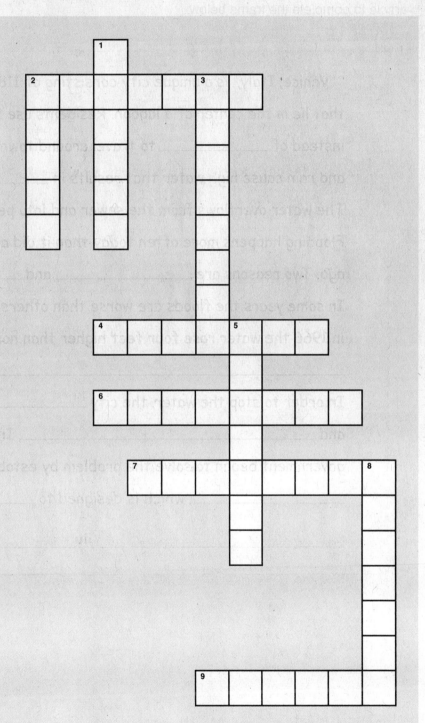

Word List

CANAL	DIVERTED	SANDBAR	DEFENSE	VANISHED
BARRIER	CHANNEL	MOBILE	LAGOON	ELEVATED

WRITING FRAME

Directions: Below is a writing frame. Use your knowledge and information from the article to complete the frame below.

Venice, Italy, is a unique city consisting of 118 small islands that lie in the center of a lagoon. Residents use _____ instead of _____ to travel around town. Changing tides and rain cause high water that results in _____. The water overflows from the sewer and into people's homes. Flooding happens more often today than it did a hundred years ago. Two reasons are _____ and _____. In some years the floods are worse than others. For example, in 1966 the water rose four feet higher than normal because

_____.

In order to stop the water, the city _____ and _____. In 2003 the government began to solve the problem by establishing the _____, which is designed to _____

_____.

TAKE A STAND

Directions: People often have different feelings, or opinions, about the same thing. A "debate" is when people argue their different ideas. A good, persuasive argument has the following:

Facts – statements that can be proven to be true.

Statistics – research from a scientific study that uses numbers.

Examples – stories from the world that support an opinion.

You and a partner are going to debate two of your other classmates. The topic you are going to debate is the following:

People should stop nature from destroying old historic places.

Decide whether you agree or disagree with this statement. Then answer these questions in order to win your debate.

1. What are your 2 strongest points to persuade the other side?
(You can do Internet research to include facts, statistics, and examples.)

A. _____

B. _____

2. What will the other side say to argue against point A?
_____
_____

3. What will the other side say to argue against point B?
_____
_____

4. What will you say to prove the other side's arguments are wrong?
_____
_____

ASSESSMENT

Comprehension: Answer the questions about the passage below.

In 2003 the government began the MOSE project. It is putting 79 hollow mobile gates at the three inlets. Normally the gates will lie flat on the sea floor and not affect the flow of water. However, during high waters managers will pump air into them. That will make them rise and form a barrier or a wall against the entering tide. High waters in Venice have become too frequent for comfort. Twenty million tourists will visit the city this year. MOSE is supposed to be finished in 2011, and then maybe high waters and the flooding will be a thing of the past.

1. Why are high waters a problem in Venice?

_____

_____

2. What are Venetians doing to stop flooding?

_____

_____

3. What was the author's purpose for writing about Venice and floods?

_____

_____

Fluency: The words in the two sentences are all connected. The sentences are also missing punctuation and capitalization. Draw slash marks (/) between the words. Then rewrite the sentence, filling in the punctuation and capitalization.

1. mostvenetiansnolongerliveonthegroundfloor

_____

_____

2. thegateswillrisewhenthelevelreachesfortythreeinchesabovenormal

_____

_____

ASSESSMENT

Fluency: Read the three sentences below. Imagine where you would pause within each sentence as you read it aloud. Draw a slash (/) mark between the phrases where you would pause. The first slash is done.

3. Natural protection / from the tides has all but vanished.

4. Two things cause the increase in high water.

5. Climate change experts predict a rise in the seas of at least 12 inches in this century.

Vocabulary: Based on what you have learned in this lesson, match the following words with their definitions. Write the letter of the definition on the blank in front of the word it defines.

1. _____ canal   **A.** disappeared

2. _____ elevated   **B.** protection

3. _____ defense   **C.** movable

4. _____ diverted   **D.** a long, narrow passage of water

5. _____ lagoon   **E.** turned away

6. _____ sandbar   **F.** a thin strip of land formed by waves

7. _____ barrier   **G.** raised or lifted up

8. _____ vanished   **H.** a wide, deep waterway

9. _____ mobile   **I.** a wall to block something

10. _____ channel   **J.** an area of shallow water separated from the sea by a strip of land

Name _____ Date _____

ANTICIPATION GUIDE

Directions: <u>Before</u> you read the article "Museum Looks for Art's Rightful Owner," read the statements below. If you agree with a statement, put a check on the line. Otherwise, leave it blank.

_____ **1.** People who dig up an old piece of art should be able to keep it.

_____ **2.** It's okay to buy art that was stolen hundreds of years ago.

_____ **3.** Very rare art should stay in the country where it was created.

Once you have checked the statements above, tell why you agreed or disagreed with each statement in the section below.

1. _____

_____

2. _____

_____

3. _____

_____

In the box below, draw a picture of what you think this article is about.

What's Happening
IN CALIFORNIA?

By Lawrence Gable
© *2010 What's Happening Publications*

Subject: Art

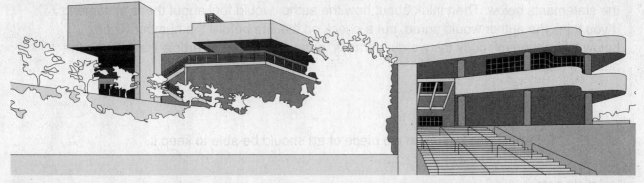

Museum Looks for Art's Rightful Owner

Running an art museum is complicated. It involves finding, buying, displaying, protecting and restoring art. It also involves recognizing provenance, the rightful ownership of works of art. The J. Paul Getty Museum in Los Angeles has had problems with that in recent years. Italy wants the museum to return some pieces.

Proving provenance is important for several reasons. Before a museum pays millions for a piece, it wants proof that it is not fake. It also does not want to buy art that has been stolen.

Wars are a source of stolen art. In World War II, for example, the Nazi government in Germany stole art from Jews and nations it conquered. Then the victorious Allies stole a million pieces from Germany. Sixty years later pieces are still being returned to their rightful owners.

The United Nations prohibits the trade of stolen art. In 1970 it defined art as "cultural property." Now 130 countries prohibit and prevent the illegal trade and ownership of art. Art experts believe that it helps. In the Iraq War, for example, looters stole 15,000 objects from the Iraq Museum in 2003. Several countries, including the U.S., returned 4,000 pieces in the years immediately after that.

It is hard to prove the provenance of ancient art. Many museums have pieces from ancient Egyptian, Greek, and Roman civilizations. In fact, thieves still excavate pieces from tombs and archaeological sites. Museums try to be careful. Even so, countries like Italy protest and want pieces back.

Italy made agreements in 2006 with several American museums. The Metropolitan Museum of Art in New York and Boston's Museum of Fine Arts returned some art. In exchange Italy promised to loan other pieces in the future. Italy also wanted 52 pieces back from the Getty. At first the museum agreed to return 26 items. They included statues, figurines and pottery.

The Getty wanted to keep two especially important pieces. "Aphrodite" is a limestone statue from the fifth century B.C. Italy claimed that this statue was excavated illegally. In 2007 the museum agreed to return it in 2010. The "Getty Bronze" is a life-sized statue of an athlete. Before the museum bought it, Italian courts had said that it did not belong to Italy. However, in 2010 an Italian court demanded that statue's return.

The Getty Museum will continue to talk with Italy about this piece. It uses art to expand the cultural knowledge of visitors. It also tries to preserve the heritage of cultures that made the art. Like other great museums, it must decide whether that also means returning even more pieces to where they came from.

Name _____ Date _____

Directions: Now that you have read "Museum Looks for Art's Rightful Owner," reread the statements below. Then think about how the author would feel about these statements. If you think the author would agree, put a check on the line before the number. Then, below the statement, copy the words, phrases, or sentences in the article that tell you the author's real views.

_____ **1.** People who dig up an old piece of art should be able to keep it.

Article notes: _____

_____

_____

_____ **2.** It's okay to buy art that was stolen hundreds of years ago.

Article notes: _____

_____

_____

_____ **3.** Very rare art should stay in the country where it was created.

Article notes: _____

_____

_____

Name _____ Date _____

PREDICTING ABC's

Directions: The article you are going to read is about "art in museums." See how many boxes you can fill in below with words about art museums. For example, put the word "painting" in the P–R box. Try to put at least one word in every box.

A–C	D–F	G–I
J–L	M–O	P–R
S–T	U–V	W–Z

TIME MY READ # 1

Directions: With a partner, you will see how many words you can read correctly in 45 seconds. As you read, your partner will put an "X" through any word read incorrectly. Then your partner will read while you keep score. When you have both read, trade your books or papers. Count the total number of words you read correctly. Write this score at the bottom of your page.

WORD COUNT

restore display protect provenance conquer prohibit Nazi looter	8
excavate allies civilization illegal threaten exchange preserve heritage	16
complicated exchange archaeological insist recognize protest expand claim	24
restore display protect provenance conquer prohibit Nazi looter	32
excavate allies civilization illegal threaten exchange preserve heritage	40
complicated exchange archaeological insist recognize protest expand claim	48
restore display protect provenance conquer prohibit Nazi looter	56
excavate allies civilization illegal threaten exchange preserve heritage	64
complicated exchange archaeological insist recognize protest expand claim	72
restore display protect provenance conquer prohibit Nazi looter	80

Number of words read correctly _____.

Name _____ Date _____

ECHO READING

Directions: Your teacher will read aloud the text below. Listen carefully. Draw lines under the words he or she groups together. The first sentence has been done for you.

Italy made agreements in 2006 with several American museums. The Metropolitan Museum of Art in New York and Boston's Museum of Fine Arts returned some art. In exchange Italy promised to loan other pieces in the future. Italy also wanted 52 pieces back from the Getty. At first the museum agreed to return 26 items. They included statues, figurines and pottery.

The Getty wanted to keep two especially important pieces. "Aphrodite" is a limestone statue from the fifth century B.C. Italy claimed that this statue had been excavated illegally. In 2007 the museum agreed to return it in 2010. The "Getty Bronze" is a life-sized statue of an athlete. Before the museum bought it, Italian courts had said that it did not belong to Italy. However, in 2010 an Italian court demanded the statue's return.

GET A CONTEXT CLUE

Directions: Below are sentences from "Museum Looks for Art's Rightful Owner." Read the sentence. Look back in the article and read the paragraph the sentence is in. Circle what you think is the best answer to each question.

"It also involves recognizing provenance, the rightful ownership of works of art."

1. The word "provenance" means:

   A. who sells art
   B. who really owns a piece of art
   C. who steals art
   D. who can buy art

"The United Nations prohibits the trade of stolen art."

2. The term "prohibits" means:

   A. likes
   B. doesn't allow
   C. allows
   D. helps

"In fact, thieves still excavate pieces from tombs and archaeological sites."

3. The word "excavate" means:

   A. buy
   B. find
   C. dig up
   D. clean

"In exchange Italy promised to loan other pieces in the future."

4. The term "exchange" means:

   A. trust
   B. trade
   C. regret
   D. time

"Italy claimed this statue was excavated illegally."

5. The word "illegally" means:

   A. quickly
   B. smoothly
   C. rightfully
   D. wrongly

"It also tries to preserve the heritage of cultures that made the art."

6. The word "preserve" means:

   A. to keep safe
   B. sell
   C. destroy
   D. buy

WORD MAP

Directions: Follow the directions to map the word in the box below.

illegal

List 2 more words that mean the same.

List 2 more examples of illegal actions.

List 2 more opposites or non-examples.

unlawful

murder

legal

Draw a picture below to help you remember the meaning.

Write a definition IN YOUR OWN WORDS.

LOOK WHO'S TALKING

Directions: Below are references from "Museum Looks for Art's Rightful Owner."
Number each paragraph. Look back in the article and re-read the paragraph in which you
find the reference. Circle what you think is the best answer to each question.

1. In the second paragraph, the word
"It" best refers to:

A. the art
B. the museum
C. Italy
D. Los Angeles

2. In paragraph four, in the sentence
"Art experts believe that it helps,"
the "it" refers to:

A. the art objects
B. the prohibition of trade
C. the selling of the art
D. the victorious Allies

3. In paragraph five, the word "It"
refers to:

A. proving who owns the art
B. excavating the tombs
C. museums being careful
D. protesting from Italy

4. In paragraph six, the word "they"
refers to:

A. what was stolen
B. who stole the pieces
C. the people of Italy
D. the Getty Museum

5. In paragraph seven in the sentence,
"Before the museum bought it,
Italian courts said that it did not
belong to Italy," the word "it"
refers to:

A. the art
B. the excavation
C. the Getty Bronze
D. the loaning of pieces in the future

6. In paragraph eight, the first use of
"It" refers to:

A. the Getty Museum
B. the country of Italy
C. the other great museums
D. the artwork

HOW'S IT ORGANIZED?

This article is organized as a problem that needs solving.

Directions: Answer these questions in the spaces at the bottom.

1. Why is provenance a problem for museums?

2. Who has this problem?

3. What has been a major cause of this problem?

4. What has the United Nations said about the problem?

5. Why is Italy involved in this problem?

6. What solutions have been tried?

7. What results have come from these solutions?

8. What problems still need to be solved?

Answers:

1.	
2.	
3.	
4.	
5.	
6.	
7.	
8.	

IS THAT A FACT?

Directions: Read the definitions of a <u>fact</u> and an <u>inference</u> below. Then read the paragraph that follows. At the bottom of the page, write an "F" on the blank if a sentence is a fact. Write an "I" if the sentence is an inference. Use the following definitions:

Fact – a statement that can be proven to be true from the article.

Inference – a guess as to what MIGHT be true.

> "The Getty will continue to talk with Italy about this piece. It uses art to expand the cultural knowledge of visitors. It also tries to preserve the heritage of cultures that made the art. Like other great museums, it must decide whether that also means returning even more pieces to where they came from."

_____ **1.** Museums try to expand their visitors' cultural knowledge through art.

_____ **2.** The Getty is concerned about Italy's wishes.

_____ **3.** The Getty Museum may have to return other pieces to other countries.

_____ **4.** The Getty would like to keep any pieces that it thinks aren't stolen.

_____ **5.** Preserving a country's heritage and culture are important.

Name _____ Date _____

MAKE A SPACE

Directions: Below are sentences that are missing punctuation and capitalization. First, draw slash marks (/) between the words. Then rewrite each sentence in the space below it, filling in the missing punctuation and capitalization.

Example:

runninganartmuseumiscomplicated

Running an art museum is complicated.

1. theunitednationsprohibitsthetradeofstolenart

_____

_____

2. themuseuminsiststhatitneverknowinglyboughtstolenpieces

_____

_____

3. warsareasourceofstolenart

_____

_____

4. infactthievesstillexcavatepiecesfromtombsandarchaeologicalsites

_____

_____

_____

TIME MY READ # 2

Directions: With a partner, you will see how many words you can read correctly in 45 seconds. As you read, your partner will put an "X" through any word read incorrectly. Then your partner will read while you keep score. When you have both read, trade your books or papers. Count the total number of words you read correctly. Write this score at the bottom of your page.

WORD COUNT

restore display protect provenance conquer prohibit Nazi looter	8
excavate allies civilization illegal threaten exchange preserve heritage	16
complicated exchange archaeological insist recognize protest expand claim	24
restore display protect provenance conquer prohibit Nazi looter	32
excavate allies civilization illegal threaten exchange preserve heritage	40
complicated exchange archaeological insist recognize protest expand claim	48
restore display protect provenance conquer prohibit Nazi looter	56
excavate allies civilization illegal threaten exchange preserve heritage	64
complicated exchange archaeological insist recognize protest expand claim	72
restore display protect provenance conquer prohibit Nazi looter	80

Number of words read correctly _____. Is the score higher

than it was in Time My Read #1?_____

WORD PARTS

Directions: A suffix is added to the end of a base word to change how it's used in a sentence. Look at the sentence below.

It also involves recognizing the rightful **ownership** of works of art.

In the word "ownership," owner is the base word. Adding **–ship** means that someone or something is, has, or possesses the base word. In this case someone possesses, or owns, the works of art. Write a definition of <u>just the base words below.</u>

1. friendship – _____

2. membership – _____

3. dictatorship – _____

4. citizenship – _____

5. companionship – _____

6. scholarship – _____

7. championship – _____

8. marksmanship – _____

9. leadership – _____

10. mentorship – _____

Directions: Draw pictures to show the meanings of 2 of these words.

SUMMARIZING ABC's

Directions: Now that you've read the article on museums that return stolen art, see how many words you can fill in the boxes below.

A–C	D–F	G–I
J–L	M–O	P–R
S–T	U–V	W–Z

"Museum Looks for Art's Rightful Owner"

SENTENCE SUMMARIES

Directions: Below are 4 key words from the article "Museum Looks for Art's Rightful Owner." Your job is to summarize, or restate, what you've learned in this article by using these 4 words or phrases in two sentences. Then, as a challenge, try to use all 4 words or phrases in one sentence to restate the article.

FOUR KEY WORDS OR PHRASES

J. Paul Getty Museum   Italy

stolen art   United Nations

Sentence Summaries:

1. _____

   _____

2. _____

   _____

Challenge Summary – (All 4 words or phrases in one sentence!)

1. _____

   _____

   _____

TAKE A STAND

Directions: People often have different feelings, or opinions, about the same thing. A "debate" is when people argue their different ideas. A good, persuasive argument has the following:

Facts – statements that can be proven to be true.

Statistics – research from a scientific study that uses numbers.

Examples – stories from the world that support an opinion.

You and a partner are going to debate two of your other classmates. The topic you are going to debate is the following:

Very rare art should stay in the country where it was created.

Decide whether you agree or disagree with this statement.
Then answer these questions in order to win your debate.

1. What are your 2 strongest points to persuade the other side?
(You can do Internet research to include facts, statistics, and examples.)

A. _____

B. _____

2. What will the other side say to argue against point A?

_____

3. What will the other side say to argue against point B?

_____

_____

4. What will you say to prove the other side's arguments are wrong?

_____

_____

_____

ASSESSMENT

Comprehension: Answer the questions about the passage below.

Running an art museum is complicated. It involves recognizing provenance, the source of works of art. Proving provenance is difficult for several reasons. Before a museum pays millions of dollars for a piece, it wants proof that it is not a fake. It also does not want to buy art that has been stolen. Wars are a source of stolen art. In World War II, for example, the Nazi government in Germany stole art from the Jews and nations it conquered. Then the victorious Allies stole millions of pieces from Germany. Still, sixty years later, pieces are being returned to their rightful owners.

1. How would you define the word "provenance"?

_____

_____

2. Why do you think countries steal art during wars?

_____

_____

3. What was the author's purpose for writing this article?

_____

_____

Fluency: The words in the two sentences are all connected. The sentences are also missing punctuation and capitalization. Draw slash marks (/) between the words. Then rewrite the sentence, filling in the punctuation and capitalization.

1. atfirstthemuseumagreedtoreturntwentysixstolenpieces

_____

_____

2. inexchangeitalyhaspromisedtostartloaningotherpiecesinthefuture

_____

_____

ASSESSMENT

Fluency: Read the three sentences below. Imagine where you would pause within each sentence as you read it aloud. Draw a slash (/) mark between the phrases where you would pause. The first slash is done.

3. Many museums / have pieces from ancient civilizations.

4. Before the museum bought it, Italian courts had said that it did not belong to Italy.

5. In fact, thieves still excavate pieces from tombs and archaeological sites.

Vocabulary: Based on what you have learned in this lesson, match the following words with their definitions. Write the letter of the definition on the blank in front of the word it defines.

1. _____ excavate   **A.** to keep safe

2. _____ dictatorship   **B.** being part of a group

3. _____ illegal   **C.** to trade

4. _____ provenance   **D.** skill in shooting a gun

5. _____ mentorship   **E.** unlawful

6. _____ exchange   **F.** to dig something out of the ground

7. _____ marksmanship   **G.** the rightful owner of a piece of art

8. _____ prohibit   **H.** being a teacher of someone

9. _____ preserve   **I.** to not allow

10. _____ membership   **J.** a government ruled by one person

Name _____ Date _____

ANTICIPATION GUIDE

Directions: <u>Before</u> you read the article "The Law Gets Tough with Paparazzi," read the statements below. If you agree with a statement, put a check on the line. Otherwise, leave it blank.

_____ **1.** Famous celebrities should not get special treatment.

_____ **2.** It's okay to take pictures of a celebrity's family.

_____ **3.** Photographers should respect everyone's privacy.

Once you have checked the statements above, tell why you agreed or disagreed with each statement in the section below.

1. _____

_____

2. _____

_____

3. _____

_____

In the box below, draw a picture of what you think this article is about.

```



```

What's Happening
IN CALIFORNIA?

By Lawrence Gable
© *2010 What's Happening Publications*

Subject: Human Rights

Some photographers try to get photos of celebrities in private or unguarded moments. Often they are just a bother, but sometimes they invade the celebrity's privacy. In 2010 California strengthened a law that protects people from these photographers called "paparazzi."

The Law Gets Tough with Paparazzi

In 1999 California created the first law in the U.S. to control paparazzi. There was great public outcry against them then, because they had played a role in the car crash that killed England's Princess Diana. Her brother criticized the press when he spoke at her funeral, which more than two billion people watched on television.

The law protects celebrities against invasion of privacy. That could be a trespass, when the photographer physically enters the celebrity's property. It could also be the use of audio or video equipment from a distance. The State updated the law again in 2006. That made paparazzi responsible for altercations that they cause.

An amendment in 2010 strengthened the law. It makes it a crime to take and sell unauthorized photos of celebrities in "personal or familial activity." It also makes it a crime for newspapers, magazines and TV shows to buy those photos. They are responsible for a paparazzi's misbehavior too. Finally, it increases the penalty for breaking the law to $50,000.

Photos of celebrities are big business. A photographer can get hundreds of thousands of dollars for a single photo. That makes them willing to invade someone's privacy. Paparazzi have trespassed at homes and schools, and at private events like funerals and weddings. They also have used their vehicles to block celebrities' vehicles and to chase them at high speeds.

Celebrities fight paparazzi in a number of ways. They use false names and secret entrances at hotels. They hire security guards. Often they hire extra cars as decoys. Some stars have released their own photos of children or weddings so that the photos from paparazzi lose their value. Finally, of course, some have taken paparazzi to court.

Privacy laws cover people differently. Ordinary citizens have the right to be free from public exposure. However, the law is different for "public figures" like movie stars, athletes and politicians. It allows public exposure, but still gives them a "reasonable expectation of privacy."

No other state has a law quite like this. Experts think that someday a court will decide whether the law is too strict. For now, though, public figures are glad that the law that protects their privacy is tougher than ever.

REACTION GUIDE

Directions: <u>Now that you have read</u> "The Law Gets Tough with Paparazzi," reread the statements below. Then think about how the author would feel about these statements. If you think the author would agree, put a check on the line before the number. Then, below the statement, copy the words, phrases, or sentences in the article that tell you the author's real views.

_____ **1.** Famous celebrities should not get special treatment.

Article notes: _____

_____

_____

_____ **2.** It's okay to take pictures of a celebrity's family.

Article notes: _____

_____

_____

_____ **3.** Photographers should respect everyone's privacy.

Article notes: _____

_____

_____

WORDSTORM

Directions: It's good to know more than just the dictionary definition of a word. A wordstorm lets you write down information that helps you understand what a word means, how it's related to other words, and how to use it in different ways.

What is the word?

privacy
_____

Copy the sentence from the text in which the word is used:

_____

_____

What are some other words or phrases that mean the same thing?

_____

What are three reasons why people's privacy needs to be respected?

1. _____ 2. _____ 3. _____

Name three people who would likely use this word other than teachers.

1. _____ 2. _____ 3. _____

Draw a picture that reminds you of the word "privacy" below:

TIME MY READ # 1

Directions: With a partner, you will see how many words you can read correctly in 45 seconds. As you read, your partner will put an "X" through any word read incorrectly. Then your partner will read while you keep score. When you have both read, trade your books or papers. Count the total number of words you read correctly. Write this score at the bottom of your page.

WORD COUNT

privacy celebrity invasion trespass physically property photographs amendment	8
strict equipment strengthens exposure audio expectation protects security	16
released criticized distance experts decoys unguarded figures tougher	24
privacy celebrity invasion trespass physically property photographs amendment	32
strict equipment strengthens exposure audio expectation protects security	40
released criticized distance experts decoys unguarded figures tougher	48
privacy celebrity invasion trespass physically property photographs amendment	56
strict equipment strengthens exposure audio expectation protects security	64
released criticized distance experts decoys unguarded figures tougher	72
privacy celebrity invasion trespass physically property photographs amendment	80

Number of words read correctly _____.

ECHO READING

Directions: When you read, you should make breaks between groups of words. As the teacher reads each phrase, repeat aloud what was read and underline that phrase. Then you will read the whole sentence aloud together. The first sentence has been underlined for you.

Paparazzi can get hundreds of thousands of dollars for a single photograph. Photos of celebrities are big business. This makes them willing to invade someone's privacy. Paparazzi have trespassed at homes and at schools, and private events like weddings and funerals. Celebrities fight paparazzi in a number of ways. They use false names and secret entrances at hotels. They hire security guards and hire extra cars as decoys. Recently some stars have released their own photos of their families at weddings and funerals so that they bring down the value of the paparazzi's pictures. Finally, some have taken the paparazzi to court.

No other state has a law quite like this. Experts think that someday the courts might think that the law is too strict. For now, though, public figures are glad that the law that protects their privacy is tougher than ever.

"The Law Gets Tough with Paparazzi"

GET A CONTEXT CLUE

Directions: Below are sentences from "The Law Gets Tough with Paparazzi." Read the sentence. Look back in the article and read the paragraph the sentence is in. Circle what you think is the best answer to each question.

"Some photographers try to get photos of celebrities in private or unguarded moments."

1. The word "unguarded" means:

    A. when they are in prison
    B. when they are careful
    C. when they are not looking
    D. when they are watchful

"There was great public outcry against them then because they had played a role in the car crash that killed England's Princess ..."

2. An "outcry" means:

    A. loud disapproval
    B. gossip
    C. warning
    D. joking

"The State updated the law again in 2006."

3. The word "updated" means:

    A. stopped
    B. judged
    C. disapproved
    D. improved as times changed

"Now a new amendment strengthens the law."

4. The word "amendment" means:

    A. a change
    B. a decision
    C. a question
    D. a position

"Often they hire extra cars as decoys."

5. The word "decoys" means:

    A. leaders
    B. followers
    C. fakes or imitations
    D. friends

"Experts think that someday courts will decide whether the law is too strict."

6. The word "experts" means:

    A. teachers
    B. parents
    C. senators
    D. people who know a subject well

WORD CHOICE

Directions: As you read this piece, you will find blanks for missing words. Three words are listed after the blank. One of these is correct. Read the rest of the sentence past the blank to figure out which is the correct word. Write it in the blank.

Some photographers try to get pictures of celebrities in private or unguarded moments. In 1999 California _____ (creating, creation, created) the first law in the U.S. to _____ (control, controlled, controlling) paparazzi. At that time there _____ (were, was, wasn't) a great public outcry against them because they _____ (has, have, had) played a role in the car crash in Paris that had killed Princess Diana of England. The law _____ (protecting, protection, protects) a celebrity against invasion of privacy. What might be considered a trespass is when a photographer _____ (enters, entering, enter) the _____ (celebrities, celebrities's, celebrity's) property without his or her permission. A new amendment _____ (makes, making, make) it a crime to sell unauthorized pictures of famous people in private or family settings. Public figures and famous people are now happy that the law is tougher than ever and that it _____ (protects, protected, protecting) their right to privacy.

LOOK WHO'S TALKING

Directions: Below are sentences from "The Law Gets Tough with Paparazzi." Number each paragraph. Look back in the article and re-read the paragraph in which you find the reference. Circle what you think is the best answer to each question.

1. In the second paragraph, the word "them" best refers to:

A. the stars
B. celebrities
C. the photographers
D. the public

2. In paragraph three, the word "it" refers to:

A. the photographers
B. the trespassing
C. the use of audio
D. the invasion of privacy

3. In paragraph four in the last sentence, "Finally, it increases the penalty for breaking the law to $50,000," the word "it" refers to:

A. the amendment
B. the use of photographs
C. the use of audio
D. the crime

4. In paragraph five, the word "they" refers to:

A. the paparazzi
B. the security guards
C. the people
D. the celebrities

5. In paragraph seven in the last sentence, the word "them" refers to:

A. the celebrities
B. the paparazzi
C. the figures
D. the citizens

6. The word "this" in the first sentence of the final paragraph refers to:

A. the problem
B. the amendment
C. the use of photographs
D. the court

NOTE MAKING

Directions: Read the key **bold** words on the left side of the chart below. Then add notes that answer the question in parentheses under the key word.

Paparazzi

(What?)

Dangerous

(Why?)

Invasion of privacy

(When)

Celebrities fight back

(How?)

Privacy laws cover

(Which people?)

IS THAT A FACT?

Directions: Read the definitions of a <u>fact</u> and an <u>inference</u> below. Then read the paragraph that follows. At the bottom of the page, write an "F" on the blank if a sentence is a fact or an "I" if it is an inference. Use the following definitions:

<u>Fact</u> – a statement that can be proven to be true from the article.

<u>Inference</u> – a guess as to what MIGHT be true.

"Privacy laws cover people differently. Ordinary citizens have the right to be free from public exposure. However, the law is different for public figures like movie stars, athletes, and politicians. It allows public exposure, but still gives them a reasonable expectation of privacy. No other state has a law quite like this. Experts think that someday a court will decide whether the law is too strict. For now though, public figures are glad that the law that protects their privacy is tougher than ever."

_____ **1.** Public figures expect to be photographed when in public.

_____ **2.** Celebrities have a reasonable expectation of privacy by law.

_____ **3.** The law might eventually be changed.

_____ **4.** California, as a state, tries to take care of its celebrities.

_____ **5.** Paparazzi have taken advantage of movie stars, athletes, and politicians.

_____ **6.** Ordinary people don't need to worry about paparazzi invading their privacy.

TIME MY READ # 2

Directions: With a partner, you will see how many words you can read correctly in 45 seconds. As you read, your partner will put an "X" through any word read incorrectly. Then your partner will read while you keep score. When you have both read, trade your books or papers. Count the total number of words you read correctly. Write this score at the bottom of your page.

WORD COUNT

privacy celebrity invasion trespass physically property photographs amendment	8
strict equipment strengthens exposure audio expectation protects security	16
released criticized distance experts decoys unguarded figures tougher	24
privacy celebrity invasion trespass physically property photographs amendment	32
strict equipment strengthens exposure audio expectation protects security	40
released criticized distance experts decoys unguarded figures tougher	48
privacy celebrity invasion trespass physically property photographs amendment	56
strict equipment strengthens exposure audio expectation protects security	64
released criticized distance experts decoys unguarded figures tougher	72
privacy celebrity invasion trespass physically property photographs amendment	80

Number of words read correctly _____. Is the score higher than it was in

Time My Read #1? _____

Name _____ Date _____

MAKE A SPACE

Directions: Below are sentences that are missing punctuation and capitalization. First, draw slash marks (/) between the words. Then rewrite each sentence in the space below it, filling in the missing punctuation and capitalization.

> Example:
>
> some/paparazzi/try/to/get/celebrities/in/uncomfortable/situations
>
> Some paparazzi try to get celebrities in uncomfortable situations.

1. sometimestheyareonlyabotherbutsometimestheyinvadepeoplesprivacy

_____

_____

2. celebritiesmayfightpaparazziinanumberofways

_____

_____

3. ordinarycitizenshavearighttobefreefrompublicexposure

_____

_____

4. itmakesitacrimefortvnewspapersandmagazinestobuythephotographs

_____

_____

WORD PARTS

Directions: A **base word** is a word that can stand alone. A **prefix** is a word part added to the beginning of a base word. In the word **retry, try** is the base word and **re-** is the prefix. The prefix **re-** means "again." Retry means "to do something again." (Sometimes the **re-** at the beginning of a word is NOT a prefix. For example, in the word repeat, you do not "peat" again.) Write 10 words that begin with the prefix **re-** on the lines below. Share the words with the rest of the class.

1. _____   6. _____

2. _____   7. _____

3. _____   8. _____

4. _____   9. _____

5. _____   10. _____

Directions: A suffix is added to the end of a word to change how it's used in a sentence. The suffix **-able** means "can be" or "made to be." In the following sentence, see how the **verb** depend, which means "to trust," becomes an **adjective** that describes the mail carrier.

Our mail carrier is very dependable, delivering the mail every day.

Think of 10 verbs you can turn into adjectives by adding the suffix **-able.** Write them on the blanks below and share them with the class.

1. _____   6. _____

2. _____   7. _____

3. _____   8. _____

4. _____   9. _____

5. _____   10. _____

PAPARAZZI WORD PUZZLE

Directions: Complete the crossword puzzle.

Across

1 to shut again

5 a change

7 loud disapproval

9 to be able to make sense of something

10 to be able to be given back

Down

2 people who know a subject well

3 the right to be left alone

4 improved as time changed

6 when no one is looking

8 a fake or imitation

Word List

RETURNABLE	AMENDMENT	OUTCRY	RECLOSE	UNGUARDED
UPDATED	PRIVACY	EXPERTS	UNDERSTANDABLE	DECOY

WRITING FRAME

Directions: Below is a writing frame. Use your knowledge and information from the article to complete the frame below.

Some photographers, or "paparazzi," try to get photos of celebrities in private or unguarded moments. Sometimes they appear at _____ _____. California created the first law to _____. The law was created because there had been public outcry about _____ _____. The new law protects celebrities against _____. Paparazzi might invade a celebrity's privacy by _____, or _____. The amendment to the law in 2010 makes it a crime to _____. Privacy laws cover people differently. For example, ordinary citizens have _____ _____. The law is different for public figures such as _____, _____, and _____. The law allows public exposure but still gives them a _____.

Name _____ Date _____

TAKE A STAND

Directions: People often have different feelings, or opinions, about the same thing. A "debate" is when people argue their different ideas. A good, persuasive argument has the following:

Facts – statements that can be proven to be true.

Statistics – research from a scientific study that uses numbers.

Examples – stories from the world that support an opinion.

You and a partner are going to debate two of your other classmates. The topic you are going to debate is the following:

> *Photographers should respect everyone's privacy.*

Decide whether you agree or disagree with this statement. Then answer these questions in order to win your debate.

1. What are your 2 strongest points to persuade the other side?
(You can do Internet research to include facts, statistics, and examples.)

A. _____

B. _____

2. What will the other side say to argue against point A?

_____

_____

3. What will the other side say to argue against point B?

_____

_____

4. What will you say to prove the other side's arguments are wrong?

_____

_____

Name _____ Date _____

ASSESSMENT

Comprehension: Answer the questions about the passage below.

The law protects celebrities against invasion of privacy. That could be a trespass, when the photographer physically enters the celebrity's property. It could also be the use of audio or video equipment from a distance. The State updated the law again in 2006. That made paparazzi responsible for altercations that they cause when they get too close. Fighting or accidents sometimes happen. Now a new amendment strengthens the law, making it a crime to sell unauthorized photos of celebrities in a personal or family activity.

1. How did the State update the law to make it stronger?

_____

_____

2. What kinds of altercations do paparazzi cause?

_____

_____

3. What was the author's purpose for writing about the paparazzi?

_____

_____

Fluency: The words in the two sentences are all connected. The sentences are also missing punctuation and capitalization. Draw slash marks (/) between the words. Then rewrite the sentence, filling in the punctuation and capitalization.

1. thelawprotectscelebritiesagainstinvasionofprivacy

_____

_____

2. italsomakesitacrimefornewspapersandmagazinestobuythepictures

_____

_____

"The Law Gets Tough with Paparazzi"

ASSESSMENT

Fluency: Read the three sentences below. Imagine where you would pause within each sentence as you read it aloud. Draw a slash (/) mark between the phrases where you would pause. The first slash is done.

3. Finally / it increases the penalty to $50,000 for breaking the law.

4. A photographer can get hundreds of thousands of dollars for a single photo.

5. However, the law is different for public figures, like movie stars, athletes and politicians.

Vocabulary: Based on what you have learned in this lesson, match the following words with their definitions. Write the letter of the definition on the blank in front of the word it defines.

1. _____ unguarded **A.** to shut again

2. _____ reclose **B.** loud disapproval

3. _____ understandable **C.** a fake or imitation

4. _____ amendment **D.** when no one is looking or watching

5. _____ outcry **E.** improved as time changed

6. _____ decoy **F.** to be able to make sense of something

7. _____ experts **G.** people who know a subject well

8. _____ returnable **H.** a change

9. _____ privacy **I.** to be able to be given back

10. _____ updated **J.** the right to be left alone

Name _____ Date _____

ANTICIPATION GUIDE

Directions: <u>Before</u> you read the article "Somalia's Problems Lead to Piracy," read the statements below. If you agree with a statement, put a check on the line. Otherwise, leave it blank.

_____ **1.** Corporations ought to be able to protect their property, even if it means killing others.

_____ **2.** Stealing is always wrong.

_____ **3.** People can do anything to survive if their government fails.

Once you have checked the statements above, tell why you agreed or disagreed with each statement in the section below.

1. _____

_____

2. _____

_____

3. _____

_____

In the box below, draw a picture of what you think this article is about.

"Somalia's Problems Lead to Piracy"

What's Happening
IN THE WORLD?

By Lawrence Gable
© 2010 What's Happening Publications

Subject: Global Issues

Somalia's Problems Lead to Piracy

For thousands of years pirates have threatened ships at sea. Ancient Greek and Roman writings tell of them. The Vikings attacked European ships in the Middle Ages, and several centuries ago pirates like Blackbeard sailed the Caribbean. In the 1990s pirates started attacking again off Somalia's coast.

This piracy really started on land. In 1991 warlords in Somalia overthrew the central government. A civil war began and the fighting continues today. Hundreds of thousands of people have died, and 3.5 million Somalis are starving. The United Nations (U.N.) sent food by land, but warlords attacked the trucks. It never reached most Somalis, so the U.N. started sending the food by sea.

Somalia's fishing industry failed at the same time. International law gives countries control of their coastal waters. However, Somalia no longer had a government to protect its waters, so other countries sent ships across the Indian Ocean to catch tuna and shark there.

In the 1990s Somali fishermen formed their own "coast guards" to stop foreign fishing. They used guns to chase them away. Then they started boarding the vessels and demanding "fees." Their piracy really began when they held the vessels and demanded a ransom from the ships' owners.

In those same years they also began hijacking the U.N.'s food ships. Some shipping companies refused to make those trips. As a result, the delivery of food became undependable and Somalis suffered.

Somalia's location puts the pirates in perfect position. The country is shaped like the number "7." Its northern coastline stretches along the Gulf of Aden, then south along the Indian Ocean. Every

year 16,000 cargo ships sail the Gulf of Aden, which connects to the Red Sea and the Suez Canal. The canal opens a shorter route between Europe and the Far East.

Somali pirates use modern equipment. They have large ships with satellite systems that locate their targets. Then they attack in small, fast boats that carry heavy machine guns and grenades. At night they race up to a ship, climb its sides and capture the crew. During the day they surround a ship, go aboard and demand a ransom.

In 2008 Somali pirates attacked more than 100 ships. They included container, cargo and cruise ships. They collected $100 million in ransom payments. At the end of the year they still held 18 of them and 300 crew members. The number of attacks rose in 2009.

In November 2008 pirates hijacked a supertanker far out in the Indian Ocean. Until then most attacks had taken place in the Gulf of Aden. It was the largest ship ever captured. They held it for several months, when they received a $3 million ransom.

That hijacking led to an international response. At least a dozen warships from different countries began to patrol the waters off Somalia. They aid vessels under attack and fight pirates. Although they had some success, they cannot control the million square miles of ocean where the pirates operate.

Piracy off Somalia does not just put ships' crews at risk. It also interrupts trade. Someday it may cause ships to sail around the southern tip of Africa instead. The biggest losers, though, are the Somali people. They are suffering and dying, and hoping for a government that will bring order to their lives.

Name _____ Date _____

REACTION GUIDE

Directions: Now that you have read "Somalia's Problems Lead to Piracy," reread the statements below. Then, think about how the author would feel about these statements. If you think the author would agree, put a check on the line before the number. Then, below the statement, copy the words, phrases, or sentences in the article that tell you the author's real views.

_____ **1.** Corporations ought to be able to protect their property, even if it means killing others.

Article notes: _____

_____

_____

_____ **2.** Stealing is always wrong.

Article notes: _____

_____

_____

_____ **3.** People can do anything to survive if their government fails.

Article notes: _____

_____

_____

"Somalia's Problems Lead to Piracy"

PREDICTING ABC's

Directions: The article you are going to read is about "pirates." See how many boxes you can fill in below with words about piracy. For example, put the word "ship" in the S–T box. Try to put at least one word in every box.

A–C	D–F	G–I
J–L	**M–O**	**P–R**
S–T	**U–V**	**W–Z**

ECHO READING

Directions: When you read, you should make breaks between groups of words. As the teacher reads each phrase, repeat aloud what was read and underline that phrase. Then you will read the whole sentence aloud together. The first sentence has been underlined for you.

In the 1990s Somali fishermen formed their own "coast guards" to stop foreign fishing. They threatened foreign boats with guns and chased them away. Then they started boarding the vessels and demanding "fees." Finally, their piracy really began when they seized the vessels and demanded a ransom from the companies that owned them.

Somalia's location puts the pirates in perfect position. The country is shaped like the number "7," and its coastline stretches almost 2,000 miles. To the north lies the Gulf of Aden. At the Horn of Africa the coastline turns south along the Indian Ocean. Every year 16,000 cargo ships sail the Gulf of Aden as they enter or leave the Red Sea. At the top of the Red Sea lies the Suez Canal, which allows ships to take a shorter route to the Mediterranean Sea.

TIME MY READ # 1

Directions: With a partner, you will see how many words you can read correctly in 45 seconds. As you read, your partner will put an "X" through any word read incorrectly. Then your partner will read while you keep score. When you have both read, trade your books or papers. Count the total number of words you read correctly. Write this score at the bottom of your page.

WORD COUNT

piracy aid starving international fishing foreign ransom demanding	8
companies delivery undependable cargo tactics aboard captured attacks	16
effort hijacking operate restore members satellite vast coastal	24
piracy aid starving international fishing foreign ransom demanding	32
companies delivery undependable cargo tactics aboard captured attacks	40
effort hijacking operate restore members satellite vast coastal	48
piracy aid starving international fishing foreign ransom demanding	56
companies delivery undependable cargo tactics aboard captured attacks	64
effort hijacking operate restore members satellite vast coastal	72
piracy aid starving international fishing foreign ransom demanding	80

Number of words read correctly _____.

GET A CONTEXT CLUE

Directions: Below are sentences from "Somalia's Problems Lead to Piracy." Read the sentence. Look back in the article. Read the paragraph the sentence is in. Circle what you think is the best answer to each question.

"In 1991 warlords in Somalia *overthrew* the central government."

1. The word "overthrew" means:

    A. got rid of; conquered
    B. utilized
    C. increase
    D. stopped

"Then they started *boarding* vessels and demanding fees."

2. The word "boarding" means:

    A. coming onto another ship
    B. buying
    C. towing
    D. responding to

"Somalia's *location* puts the pirates in perfect position."

3. The word "location" means:

    A. government
    B. boats
    C. attitude
    D. place

"The canal opens a shorter *route* between Europe and the Far East."

4. The word "route" means:

    A. course or way
    B. person
    C. ship
    D. time

"During the day they surround a ship, go aboard and demand a *ransom*."

5. The word "ransom" means:

    A. meal
    B. money for something stolen
    C. release
    D. celebration

"Although they had some success, they cannot control the million square miles of ocean where the pirates *operate*."

6. The word "operate" means:

    A. go to school
    B. do surgery
    C. commit their crimes
    D. vacation

Name _____ Date _____

Directions: As you read this piece, you will find blanks for missing words. Three words are listed after the blank. One of these is correct. <u>Read the rest of the sentence past the blank to figure out which is the correct word</u>. Write it in the blank.

Pirates have operated on many oceans for many years. But recently a new piracy problem has _____ (developing, develops, developed) off the waters of Somalia. The country of Somalia _____ (lies, lays, laying) in a perfect position because of its vantage point on the _____ (continent, country, continental) of Africa. When _____ (their, they're, there) fishing industry failed, the Somalis _____ (formed, forming, formation) their own "national guard" and started _____ (chase, chasing, chased) foreign fishermen away. Then, they started _____ (seize, sized, seizing) other country's vessels and _____ (demand, demanding, demands) that the owners pay a ransom.

Also in 1991, they _____ (began, begin, begun) to seize United Nations ships containing food. This action _____ (prevented, prevention, prevents) the country of Somalia from getting food to its starving people. The pirates use modern technology such as _____ (satellite, starlights, satellites) to locate ships that they attack. At night they _____ (racing, raced, race) up to the ship in small boats.

Name _____ Date _____

LOOK WHO'S TALKING

Directions: Below are sentences from "Somalia's Problems Lead to Piracy." Number each paragraph. Look back in the article and re-read the paragraph in which you find the reference. Circle what you think is the best answer to each question.

1. In paragraph two, the word "it" best refers to:

A. the piracy
B. the food from the U.N.
C. the trucks
D. the U.N.

2. In paragraph three, the word "its" refers to:

A. the fishing industry
B. the pirates
C. the country of Somalia
D. the United Nations

3. In paragraph four, the word "their" refers to:

A. the fishermen
B. the pirates
C. the fishing industry
D. the people of Somalia

4. In paragraph eight, the word "they" refers to:

A. the ships that were attacked
B. the pirates who attacked
C. the people
D. the hostages

5. In paragraph nine, the word "it" in the last sentence refers to:

A. the money
B. the super-tanker
C. the Indian Ocean
D. the ransom

6. In the last sentence of paragraph eleven, the words "they" and "their" refer to:

A. the Somali people
B. the pirates
C. the ships
D. the people held for ransom

Name _____ Date _____

HOW'S IT ORGANIZED?

This article is organized as a problem that needs solving.

Directions: Answer these questions in the spaces at the bottom.

1. What is the problem?

2. Why did this problem off Somalia's coast begin?

3. Why did Somalia's fishermen form "coast guards"?

4. How does this problem affect other countries?

5. Who is trying to solve the problem?

6. What results might come, or have come, from these solutions?

7. Do the solutions cause new problems? If so, what problems?

Answers:

1.	
2.	
3.	
4.	
5.	
6.	
7.	

IS THAT A FACT?

Directions: Read the definitions of a <u>fact</u> and an <u>inference</u> below. Then read the paragraph that follows. At the bottom of the page, write an "F" on the blank if a sentence is a fact. Write an "I" if the sentence is an inference. Use the following definitions:

<u>Fact</u> – a statement that can be proven to be true from the article.

<u>Inference</u> – a guess as to what MIGHT be true.

> "The hijacking of a Saudi supertanker led to an international effort against piracy off Africa's coast. At least a dozen warships from different countries began to patrol the waters off Somalia. They have international authority to come to the aid of vessels under attack and to fight pirates. Quickly they sank some boats and captured pirates, but they cannot control the millions of square miles of ocean where pirates operate."

_____ **1.** Before the large Saudi tanker was hijacked, most countries handled the problem on their own.

_____ **2.** Different countries are using warships to patrol the waters off the Somali coast.

_____ **3.** Pirates operate in too large an area to really prevent all attacks.

_____ **4.** Combating the piracy problem can lead to violence.

_____ **5.** Stopping the piracy from Somalia will take some time.

_____ **6.** The Somali government cannot control the pirates that come from their country.

Name _____ Date _____

MAKE A SPACE

Directions: Below are sentences that are missing punctuation and capitalization. First, draw slash marks (/) between the words. Then rewrite each sentence in the space below it, filling in the missing punctuation and capitalization.

Example:

in/the/1990s/somali/fishermen/formed/their/own/coast/guards/to/stop/

foreign/fishing

In the 1990s Somali fishermen formed their own "coast guards" to stop

foreign fishing.

1. theysailouttoseainlargeshipsthattheyhavecapturedbefore

_____

_____

2. internationallawgivescountriescontrolofthecoastalwaters

_____

_____

3. nowatleastadozenwarshipspatrolthewatersoffsomalia

_____

_____

4. somaliasfishingindustryfailedatthesametime

_____

_____

TIME MY READ # 2

Directions: With a partner, you will see how many words you can read correctly in 45 seconds. As you read, your partner will put an "X" through any word read incorrectly. Then your partner will read while you keep score. When you have both read, trade your books or papers. Count the total number of words you read correctly. Write this score at the bottom of your page.

WORD COUNT

piracy aid starving international fishing foreign ransom demanding	8
companies delivery undependable cargo tactics aboard captured attacks	16
effort hijacking operate restore members satellite vast coastal	24
piracy aid starving international fishing foreign ransom demanding	32
companies delivery undependable cargo tactics aboard captured attacks	40
effort hijacking operate restore members satellite vast coastal	48
piracy aid starving international fishing foreign ransom demanding	56
companies delivery undependable cargo tactics aboard captured attacks	64
effort hijacking operate restore members satellite vast coastal	72
piracy aid starving international fishing foreign ransom demanding	80

Number of words read correctly _____. Is the score higher

than it was in Time My Read #1?_____

WORD PARTS

Directions: The Latin root "civil" means *citizen*. Read the definitions below. Then draw a picture of what each word means in the box.

1. citizen – (noun) a resident of a country who can vote and is protected by that country's government and armed forces.

2. civilian – (noun) a person who is not in the military.

3. civil – (adjective) polite; behaving in a proper or well-mannered way

citizen	civilian	civil

Directions: The Latin root "navis" means *ship*. Read the sentences below. Using the clues in the sentences, write a definition on the back for each underlined word that begins with "nav."

1. The harbor was filled with warships from the enemy's navy, so the people of the city were scared.

2. When my father drives us in the car on trips, my mom acts as the navigator, looking at the map to tell dad where to turn.

3. The sailor put on his naval uniform when he was ready to go on board the ship for a voyage.

4. The captain of the large supertanker was a good sailor because he could navigate the ship under the low bridge and not hit anything.

Name _____ Date _____

SUMMARIZING ABC's

Directions: Now that you've read the article about Somalia's pirates, see how many words you can fill in the boxes below.

A–C	D–F	G–I
J–L	**M–O**	**P–R**
S–T	**U–V**	**W–Z**

SENTENCE SUMMARIES

Directions: Below are 4 key words from the article "Somalia's Problems Lead to Piracy." Your job is to summarize, or restate, what you've learned in this article by using these 4 words or phrases in two sentences. Then, as a challenge, try to use all 4 words or phrases in one sentence to restate the article.

FOUR KEY WORDS OR PHRASES

ransom   Somalia's civil war

piracy   international effort

Sentence Summaries:

1. _____

   _____

2. _____

   _____

Challenge Summary (All 4 words or phrases in one sentence!)

1. _____

   _____

   _____

TAKE A STAND

Directions: People often have different feelings, or opinions, about the same thing. A "debate" is when people argue their different ideas. A good, persuasive argument has the following:

Facts – statements that can be proven to be true.

Statistics – research from a scientific study that uses numbers.

Examples – stories from the world that support an opinion.

You and a partner are going to debate two of your other classmates. The topic you are going to debate is the following:

Stealing is always wrong.

Decide whether you agree or disagree with this statement.
Then answer these questions in order to win your debate.

1. What are your 2 strongest points to persuade the other side?
(Feel free to do Internet research to include facts, statistics, and examples.)

A. _____

B. _____

2. What will the other side say to argue against point A?

_____

3. What will the other side say to argue against point B?

_____

_____

4. What will you say to prove the other side's arguments are wrong?

_____

_____

_____

ASSESSMENT

Comprehension: Answer the questions about the passage below.

The piracy off Somalia's coast really started on land. In 1991 warlords in Somalia overthrew the central government. A civil war began and the fighting continues today. Hundreds of thousands of people have died, and 3.5 million Somalis are starving. The United Nations (U.N.) sent food by land, but warlords attacked the trucks. It never reached most Somalis, so the U.N. started sending the food by sea.

Somalia's fishing industry failed at the same time. The country no longer had a government to protect its waters, so other countries sent ships across the Indian Ocean to catch tuna and shark there.

1. What are some of the reasons why piracy occurs in Somalia?

_____

_____

2. What was the author's purpose for writing about Somalia's pirates?

_____

_____

Fluency: The words in the two sentences are all connected. The sentences are also missing punctuation and capitalization. Draw slash marks (/) between the words. Then rewrite the sentence, filling in the punctuation and capitalization.

1. somaliasfishingindustryfailedatthesametime

_____

_____

2. finallytheirpiracyreallybeganwhentheyseizedthevesselsforaransom

_____

_____

ASSESSMENT

Fluency: Read the three sentences below. Imagine where you would pause within each sentence as you read it aloud. Draw a slash (/) mark between the phrases where you would pause. The first slash is done.

3. The country / is shaped like a "7," and it has miles of coastline.

4. Every year 16,000 cargo ships sail the Gulf of Aden as they enter or leave the Red Sea.

5. In the 1990s Somali fishermen formed their own "coast guards" to stop foreign fishing.

Vocabulary: Based on what you have learned in this lesson, match the following words with their definitions. Write the letter of the definition on the blank in front of the word it defines.

1. _____ overthrew

2. _____ civilian

3. _____ route

4. _____ navy

5. _____ civil

6. _____ navigator

7. _____ ransom

8. _____ navigate

9. _____ boarding

10. _____ location

A. behaving in a well-mannered way

B. a place

C. a large group of warships

D. climbing onto a ship

E. a person who is not in the military

F. course or way

G. to direct a boat or other vehicle

H. got rid of; conquered

I. money demanded for something stolen

J. the person who directs a boat or other vehicle

Name _____ Date _____

ANTICIPATION GUIDE

Directions: <u>Before</u> you read the article "Special Olympics Changes Lives," read the statements below. If you agree with a statement, put a check on the line. Otherwise, leave it blank.

_____ **1.** People who are intellectually disabled can't do very much.

_____ **2.** Every athlete is a winner.

_____ **3.** Schools should not allow disabled students to play major sports, such as varsity football, basketball and volleyball.

Once you have checked the statements above, tell why you agreed or disagreed with each statement in the section below.

1. _____
_____

2. _____
_____

3. _____
_____

In the box below, draw a picture of what you think this article is about.

By Lawrence Gable
© *2010 What's Happening Publications*

Subject: Sports

Special Olympics Changes Lives

In January 2005 Rosemary Kennedy died at age 86. She certainly was not famous like her brother, John F. Kennedy. She was intellectually disabled and lived in an institution most of her life. People know something of her, though. She was the inspiration for Special Olympics.

Rosemary's sister, Eunice Kennedy Shriver, was the founder of Special Olympics. In their youth she and Rosemary played games together. Mrs. Shriver saw that people with intellectual disabilities could compete and have fun. She also saw that too many of them lived in isolation.

The idea for Special Olympics began in the early 1960s. Mrs. Shriver started a summer day camp for 35 people. She believed that physical exercise would improve their fitness and motor skills. She also felt that they could learn the rules for team sports.

In 1968 Mrs. Shriver organized the first World Games. Around 1,000 athletes from 26 states and Canada competed in track and field, swimming and floor hockey. Two years later the number of athletes doubled. They came from all 50 states, the District of Columbia, Puerto Rico and France.

Special Olympics has spread across the world. Now 151 countries sponsor more than 20,000 competitions. Each year 1.4 million athletes compete in 26 sports. Recent World Games have had 7, 000 athletes. The summer and winter games alternate every two years. Winter sports include skiing, skating, snowboarding, snowshoeing and floor hockey.

Every athlete recites an oath before major competitions. It reads: "Let me win. But if I cannot win, let me be brave in the attempt." Officials believe that every athlete there is a winner. The games focus totally on the athletes, not on flags and national anthems.

Social interaction is a large part of Special Olympics. The athletes make new friends. Beyond that, families have learned to be proud of their disabled relatives. Not even 20 parents attended the first games in 1968. Now, however, parents are a large part of the 750,000 volunteers who organize competitions.

Special Olympics has improved athletes' health. For a long time doctors believed that mental retardation shortened lives. Special Olympics showed them that the real problem was just poor health care. Often families were too ashamed to seek regular medical attention. Many institutions also did not give regular medical and dental care.

In 1995 officials made an astounding discovery. Doctors, dentists and optometrists examined the athletes at the World Summer Games. They had to send almost 20% of the athletes to emergency rooms for medical care. Now a private doctor gives permission for an athlete to compete.

The doctor also sends an athlete's medical history so that coaches can keep the athletes safe.

There are eight million intellectually disabled people in U.S. Like everybody else, they want to succeed and be accepted by their communities. Special Olympics programs develop skills and pride in their athletes. As they do, they are also changing public attitudes about the intellectually disabled.

REACTION GUIDE

Directions: Now that you have read "Special Olympics Changes Lives," reread the statements below. Then think about how the author would feel about these statements. If you think the author would agree, put a check on the line before the number. Then, below the statement, copy the words, phrases, or sentences in the article that tell you the author's real views.

_____ **1.** People who are intellectually disabled can't do very much.

Article notes: _____

_____

_____

_____ **2.** Every athlete is a winner.

Article notes: _____

_____

_____

_____ **3.** Schools should not allow disabled students to play major sports, such as varsity football, basketball and volleyball.

Article notes: _____

_____

_____

WORDSTORM

Directions: It's good to know more than just the dictionary definition of a word. A wordstorm lets you write down information that helps you understand what a word means, how it's related to other words, and how to use it in different ways.

What is the word?

athletes
_____

Copy the sentence from the text in which the word is used:

_____

_____

What are some other words or phrases that mean the same thing?

_____

What are three examples of athletes?

1. _____ 2. _____ 3. _____

Name three people who would likely use this word other than

teachers.

1. _____ 2. _____ 3. _____

Draw a picture that reminds you of the word "**athlete**" below:

TIME MY READ # 1

Directions: With a partner, you will see how many words you can read correctly in 45 seconds. As you read, your partner will put an "X" through any word read incorrectly. Then your partner will read while you keep score. When you have both read, trade your books or papers. Count the total number of words you read correctly. Write this score at the bottom of your page.

WORD COUNT

fitness disabled alternate intellectually exercise motor athletes track	8
swimming sponsor interaction retardation medical astounding private physical	16
history isolation institution competition problem dentists emergency organize	24
fitness disabled alternate intellectually exercise motor athletes track	32
swimming sponsor interaction retardation medical astounding private physical	40
history isolation institution competition problem dentists emergency organize	48
fitness disabled alternate intellectually exercise motor athletes track	56
swimming sponsor interaction retardation medical astounding private physical	64
history isolation institution competition problem dentists emergency organize	72
fitness disabled alternate intellectually exercise motor athletes track	80

Number of words read correctly _____.

Name _____ Date _____

Directions: When you read, you should make breaks between groups of words. As the teacher reads each phrase, repeat aloud what was read and underline that phrase. Then you will read the whole sentence aloud together. The first sentence has been underlined for you.

Social interaction is a large part of the Special Olympics. The athletes make new friends. Beyond that, families have learned to be proud of their disabled relatives. Not even 20 parents attended the first games in 1968. Now, however, parents are a large part of the volunteers who organize the competitions.

Special Olympics have improved the athletes' health. For a long time doctors believed that mental retardation shortened lives. The Special Olympics showed them that the real problem was just poor health care. Often families were too ashamed to seek regular medical attention. Many institutions also did not give regular medical and dental care.

In 1995 officials made an astounding discovery. Doctors, dentists and optometrists examined athletes at the World Summer Games. They had to send almost 20% of the athletes to emergency rooms for medical care. Today a private doctor gives permission for an athlete to compete. They also send a medical history for each competitor so that the athletes can be kept safe.

GET A CONTEXT CLUE

Directions: Below are sentences from "Special Olympics Change Lives." Read the sentence. Look back in the article and read the paragraph the sentence is in. Circle what you think is the best answer to each question.

"People used to think that because someone was disabled, he or she had limited *intellectual* capability."

1. The word "intellectual" means:

   A. speaking
   B. hearing
   C. intelligence or thinking
   D. physical strength

"She believed that physical exercise would improve their fitness and *motor skills.*"

2. The phrase "motor skills" is best described as:

   A. the ability to move muscles
   B. working with cars
   C. intelligence
   D. how to think about something

"The Special Olympics changed public *attitude* about the disabled."

3. The word "attitude" means:

   A. anger
   B. understanding
   C. feeling or opinion
   D. conversation

"Social *interaction* is a large part of Special Olympics."

4. The word "interaction" means:

   A. working together
   B. waiting to act on something
   C. doing something by yourself
   D. confusion

"She was intellectually *disabled* and lived in an institution most of her life."

5. The word "disabled" means:

   A. growing quickly
   B. unable to decide
   C. intelligent
   D. handicapped

"Each athlete *recites* an oath before major competitions."

6. The word "recites" means:

   A. saying something that has been written
   B. singing
   C. seeing something differently
   D. poems

WORD CHOICE

Directions: As you read this piece, you will find blanks for missing words. Three words are listed after the blank. One of these is correct. <u>Read the rest of the sentence past the blank to figure out which is the correct word</u>. Write it in the blank.

The idea for the Special Olympics came about in the 1960s. Mrs. Shriver _____ (begin, began, begun) to understand that people with disabilities could compete and _____ (have, having, had) fun. She _____ (believing, believes, believed) that physical exercise would _____ (improve, improving, improved) disabled people's motor skills.

In 1968 she (organizing, organizer, organized) the first World Games. Around 1,000 _____ (athletes, atheletes, athletics) from 26 states and Canada _____ (competing, competition, competed) in track and field, swimming and floor hockey. Two years later the number of competitors _____ (doubling, doubled, double).

Each competitor _____ (recites, recite, reciting) an oath before major events. It _____ (reads, read, readers): "Let me win. But if I cannot win, let me be brave in the attempt." Officials _____ (believing, belief, believe) that every athlete is a winner. The games focus totally on the athletes and not on the flags or the national anthems.

LOOK WHO'S TALKING

Directions: Below are sentences from "Special Olympics Changes Lives." Number each paragraph. Look back in the article and re-read the paragraph in which you find the reference. Circle what you think is the best answer to each question.

1. **In paragraph two, the word "their" refers to:**

   A. the people with disabilities
   B. the athletes
   C. the relatives who compete
   D. none of the above

2. **In the second paragraph, the word "them" best refers to:**

   A. Rosemary Kennedy and Eunice Shriver
   B. people with disabilities
   C. Rosemary and John Kennedy
   D. Eunice Shriver and John Kennedy

3. **In paragraph four, the word "they" refers to:**

   A. the athletes
   B. the families
   C. the public
   D. the doctors

4. **In paragraph seven, the word "their" refers to:**

   A. the athletes
   B. the doctors
   C. the families
   D. the officials

5. **In paragraph eight the first use of the word "them" refers to:**

   A. the doctors
   B. the officials
   C. the intellectually disabled
   D. the families

6. **In paragraph ten, the last use of the word "they" refers to:**

   A. the games
   B. the athletes
   C. the doctors
   D. the officials

Name _____ Date _____

NOTE MAKING

Directions: Read the key words on the left side of the chart below. Then add notes that answer the question in parentheses under the key word.

Eunice Kennedy Shriver (Who?)	
Special Olympics (For whom?)	
Oath (Which?)	
Social Interaction (What?)	
Improved health (Why?)	

IS THAT A FACT?

Directions: Read the definitions of a <u>fact</u> and an <u>inference</u> below. Then read the paragraph that follows. At the bottom of the page, write an "F" on the blank if a sentence is a fact or an "I" if it is an inference. Use the following definitions:

<u>Fact</u> – a statement that can be proven to be true from the article.

<u>Inference</u> – a guess as to what MIGHT be true.

"The Special Olympics has spread across world. Now 151 countries sponsor more than 20,000 athletes. Each year 1.4 million athletes compete in twenty- six sports. Recent World Games have had 7,000 athletes. The summer and winter games alternate every two years. There are eight million intellectually disabled people in the U.S. Like everybody else, they want to succeed and be accepted by their communities. Special Olympics programs develop skills and pride in their athletes. As they do, they are also changing public attitudes about the intellectually disabled."

_____ **1.** The Special Olympics has experienced amazing growth.

_____ **2.** Participation in the Special Olympics has helped people understand more about people who are disabled.

_____ **3.** There are twenty-six sports in the Special Olympics.

_____ **4.** The public needed to become more aware of people with disabilities.

_____ **5.** There are many disabled people who strongly benefit from these programs.

_____ **6.** The disabled want to be accepted by their communities.

MAKE A SPACE

Directions: Below is a paragraph that is missing punctuation and capitalization. First, draw slash marks (/) between the words. Then rewrite each sentence in the space below it, filling in the missing punctuation and capitalization.

Example:

the/idea/for/the/special/olympics/began/in/the/1960s

The idea for the Special Olympics began in the 1960s.

1. thespecialolympicsprogramsdevelopskillsandprideintheirathletes

_____

_____

2. thespecialolympicshasspreadallaroundtheworld

_____

_____

3. thesportsincludeskiingskatingsnowboardingandfloorhockey

_____

_____

4. mrsshriverbelievedthatphysicalexerciseimprovedmotorskills

_____

_____

TIME MY READ # 2

Directions: With a partner, you will see how many words you can read correctly in 45 seconds. As you read, your partner will put an "X" through any word read incorrectly. Then your partner will read while you keep score. When you have both read, trade your books or papers. Count the total number of words you read correctly. Write this score at the bottom of your page.

WORD COUNT

fitness disabled alternate intellectually exercise motor athletes track	8
swimming sponsor interaction retardation medical astounding private physical	16
history isolation institution competition problem dentists emergency organize	24
fitness disabled alternate intellectually exercise motor athletes track	32
swimming sponsor interaction retardation medical astounding private physical	40
history isolation institution competition problem dentists emergency organize	48
fitness disabled alternate intellectually exercise motor athletes track	56
swimming sponsor interaction retardation medical astounding private physical	64
history isolation institution competition problem dentists emergency organize	72
fitness disabled alternate intellectually exercise motor athletes track	80

Number of words read correctly _____. Is the score higher

than it was in Time My Read #1? _____

WORD PARTS

Directions: A **base word** is a word that can stand alone. A **prefix** is a word part added to the beginning of a base word. For example, in the word **disabled, able** is the base word and **dis-** is the prefix added at the beginning. The prefix **dis** means "not" or "away." *Disabled* describes something or someone that does not work correctly or is not able to do something. (Sometimes the **dis** at the beginning of a word is NOT a prefix. For example, the word *distant* does not mean to "not tant." "Tant" is not a word.)

Write a definition for the words below on the line. Try <u>not</u> to use the base word in the definition. If you don't know the base word, look it up in a dictionary or ask a partner.

1. disagree – _____

2. disrespect – _____

3. disbelief – _____

4. dislike – _____

5. discontent – _____

6. discomfort – _____

7. dishonest – _____

8. disorder – _____

9. dishonor – _____

10. disloyal – _____

11. distrust – _____

12. distaste – _____

SPECIAL OLYMPICS WORD PUZZLE

Directions: Complete the crossword puzzle.

Across

4 not happy

6 a feeling or opinion

7 to disgrace or bring shame to someone

8 to speak aloud something that is written

9 to look at with doubt or suspicion

10 intelligence or thinking

Down

1 handicapped

2 to not care for something

3 untruthful

5 working together

Word List

DISHONOR	INTERACTION	DISHONEST	DISCONTENT	DISABLED
INTELLECTUAL	DISTRUST	DISLIKE	ATTITUDE	RECITE

WRITING FRAME

Directions: Below is a writing frame. Use your knowledge and information from the article to complete the frame below.

The Special Olympics was created by _____
in 1960. She created the Special Olympics because _____
_____. In 1968
Mrs. Shriver _____.
At that event around 1,000 _____ from
_____ and _____ competed.
Two years later _____. An
important part of the Special Olympics is the social interaction
because _____.

Special Olympics has improved the _____
_____. Before, families were ashamed
to _____. As a result, the
disabled _____. The athletes
who participate in the Special Olympics benefit because they
_____, and they _____
_____.

TAKE A STAND

Directions: People often have different feelings, or opinions, about the same thing. A "debate" is when people argue their different ideas. A good, persuasive argument has the following:

Facts – statements that can be proven to be true.

Statistics – research from a scientific study that uses numbers.

Examples – stories from the world that support an opinion.

You and a partner are going to debate two of your other classmates. The topic you are going to debate is the following:

Schools should not allow disabled students to play major sports.

Decide whether you agree or disagree with this statement. Then answer these questions in order to win your debate.

1. What are your 2 strongest points to persuade the other side?
(You can do Internet research to include facts, statistics, and examples.)

A. _____

B. _____

2. What will the other side say to argue against point A?

_____

3. What will the other side say to argue against point B?

_____

_____

4. What will you say to prove the other side's arguments are wrong?

_____

_____

ASSESSMENT

Comprehension: Answer the questions about the passage below.

The Special Olympics began in the 1960s. Eunice Shriver was the founder and the inspiration. She started a summer day camp for 35 people. She believed that physical exercise and fitness would improve motor skills and the lives of people with intellectual disabilities. She also felt that they could learn the rules of team sports.

Every athlete recites an oath before every event. It reads: "Let me win. But if I cannot win, let me be brave in the attempt." Officials believe that every athlete there is a winner. The games focus totally on the athletes, not on flags or national anthems.

1. What might be one of the benefits to athletes in the Special Olympics?

_____

_____

2. What do you think is the purpose in having athletes recite the oath?

_____

_____

3. What was the author's purpose for writing about Special Olympics?

_____

_____

Fluency: The words in the two sentences are all connected. The sentences are also missing punctuation and capitalization. Draw slash marks (/) between the words. Then rewrite the sentence, filling in the punctuation and capitalization.

1. socialinteractionisalargepartofthespecialolympics

_____

_____

2. specialolympicsshowedthemthattherealproblemwasjustpoorhealth

_____

_____

ASSESSMENT

Fluency: Read the three sentences below. Imagine where you would pause within each sentence as you read it aloud. Draw a slash (/) mark between the phrases where you would pause. The first slash is done.

3. There / are eight million intellectually disabled people in the U.S.

4. For a long time doctors believed that mental retardation shortened lives.

5. Like everybody else they want to be accepted by their communities.

Vocabulary: Based on what you have learned in this lesson, match the following words with their definitions. Write the letter of the definition on the blank in front of the word it defines.

1. _____ recite   **A.** a feeling or opinion

2. _____ distrust   **B.** not happy

3. _____ attitude   **C.** intelligence or thinking

4. _____ dislike   **D.** untruthful

5. _____ dishonor   **E.** to not care for something

6. _____ intellectual   **F.** handicapped

7. _____ disabled   **G.** to look at with doubt or suspicion

8. _____ dishonest   **H.** working together

9. _____ interaction   **I.** to speak aloud something that is written

10. _____ discontent   **J.** to disgrace or bring shame on someone

Name _____ Date _____

ANTICIPATION GUIDE

Directions: <u>Before</u> you read the article "Bike Sharing Gets Rolling," read the statements below. If you agree with a statement, put a check on the line. Otherwise, leave it blank.

_____ **1.** People in cities are willing to share things.

_____ **2.** If bikes were free to use in cities, people would steal them.

_____ **3.** Cities should not allow cars in their downtown areas.

Once you have checked the statements above, tell why you agreed or disagreed with each statement in the section below.

1. _____

_____

2. _____

_____

3. _____

_____

In the box below, draw a picture of what you think this article is about.

What's Happening
IN THE WORLD?

By Lawrence Gable
© 2010 What's Happening Publications

Subject: Environment

Bike Sharing Gets Rolling

Cities around the world are struggling with traffic in their downtown areas. Traffic jams waste people's time, and they fill the areas with noise and pollution. Some European cities have improved things through bike sharing programs. Their success is leading to more programs in Europe and North America too.

Bike sharing began in the Netherlands. In 1968 Amsterdam's "White Bicycles" plan put simple bicycles around the city. Residents could use a bike for free and then leave it for someone else to use. However, within a month people had stolen most of the bikes or thrown them into the canals.

Programs like Amsterdam's asked too little of the riders. In 1994 Portland, Oregon, started one like Amsterdam's. Its "Yellow Bike Project" fit the city's green image nicely. It was popular, but thieves and vandals also brought that program to an end.

Then bike sharing programs started to require some sort of payment. In 1995 Copenhagen, Denmark, put locked bikes at stations around the city. Riders used coins to unlock the bikes, and they got their money back when they returned the bikes. The program still exists today. Thieves do not steal the bikes because they look different from standard bikes and have different parts.

New bike sharing programs use high-tech methods. Some take credit cards. Others use electronic smart cards at computerized bike stands. Some even send text messages with the code that unlocks a bike. There are few problems with theft, because the programs know who the riders are.

The best of the new programs began in 2007 in Paris, France. It began with 10,000 bikes and was successful from the start. In the first 40 days people made two million trips, and in the first year they made 29 million. It grew to 20,000 silver bikes at 1,450 stations across the city.

Paris covers its costs in a number of ways. Riders use a credit card to pay about $1.50 for a day. Also, more than 200,000 people have annual memberships that cost only $43. An advertising company supports the program in exchange for ad space on city-owned places like bus stops. Finally, thieves do not steal the bikes because of global positioning and anti-theft devices.

In August 2008 Washington, D.C., became the first major American city with bike sharing. "SmartBike DC" has 120 red, three-speed bicycles at ten stations downtown. Quickly the program had 900 members. They swipe a magnetic membership card that unlocks a bike and assigns it to them for three hours.

Canada is also setting up programs in its cities. In April 2009 Montreal opened an environmentally friendly new program. "Bixi" (from "bike" and "taxi") has recyclable aluminum bikes and stations. The electronic system for locking and paying for bikes at the stations runs on solar power. Radio frequency ID tags prevent theft of the 2,400 bikes.

Bike sharing programs are finding their place in transportation. Residents and visitors are saving money on gas and saving time on short trips. The exercise they get makes them healthier, and the cities get healthier too. As these programs grow, they create a cleaner, more peaceful environment by reducing traffic, noise and pollution.

REACTION GUIDE

Directions: Now that you have read "Bike Sharing Gets Rolling," reread the statements below. Then think about how the author would feel about these statements. If you think the author would agree, put a check on the line before the number. Then, below the statement, copy the words, phrases, or sentences in the article that tell you the author's real views.

_____ **1.** People in cities are willing to share things.

Article notes: _____

_____

_____

_____ **2.** If bikes were free to use in cities, people would steal them.

Article notes: _____

_____

_____

_____ **3.** Cities should not allow cars in their downtown areas.

Article notes: _____

_____

_____

PREDICTING ABC's

Directions: The article you are going to read is about "traffic in cities." See how many words you can fill in below about large amounts of cars, buses, bikes, etc. in cities. For example, put the word "accident" in the A–C box. Try to put at least one word in every box.

A–C	D–F	G–I
J–L	**M–O**	**P–R**
S–T	**U–V**	**W–Z**

TIME MY READ # 1

Directions: With a partner, you will see how many words you can read correctly in 45 seconds. As you read, your partner will put an "X" through any word read incorrectly. Then your partner will read while you keep score. When you have both read, trade your books or papers. Count the total number of words you read correctly. Write this score at the bottom of your page.

WORD COUNT

stations advertising exchange anti-theft Bixi electronic recyclable steal	8
residents popular unlock high-tech membership annual aluminum speed	16
vandals thieves computerized standard credit European struggling plan	24
stations advertising exchange anti-theft Bixi electronic recyclable steal	32
residents popular unlock high-tech membership annual aluminum speed	40
vandals thieves computerized standard credit European struggling plan	48
stations advertising exchange anti-theft Bixi electronic recyclable steal	56
residents popular unlock high-tech membership annual aluminum speed	64
vandals thieves computerized standard credit European struggling plan	72
stations advertising exchange anti-theft Bixi electronic recyclable steal	80

Number of words read correctly _____.

ECHO READING

Directions: Your teacher will read aloud the text below. Listen carefully. Draw lines under the words he or she groups together. The first sentence has been done for you.

Cities around the world are struggling with traffic jams in their downtown areas. Traffic jams waste people's time and they fill the area with noise and pollution. Some European cities have improved things through bike sharing, and their success is leading to more programs in Europe and North America.

Bike sharing programs use high-tech methods. Some use credit cards and some use smart-cards at computerized bike stands. Some even send text messages with a code that unlocks the bike. There are few problems with theft because the program knows who the bike riders are.

GET A CONTEXT CLUE

Directions: Below are sentences from "Bike Sharing Gets Rolling." Read the sentence. Look back in the article and read the paragraph the sentence is in. Circle what you think is the best answer to each question.

*"**Residents** could use a bike for free and then leave it for someone else to use."*

1. The word "residents" means:

    A. pedestrians
    B. people who live in an area
    C. office people
    D. passengers

"Then bike sharing programs started to *require* some form of payment."

2. The word "require" means:

    A. to need; must have
    B. having choice
    C. no limits
    D. undecided

"There are fewer problems with *theft* because the programs know who the riders are."

3. The word "theft" best means:

    A. accidents
    B. citizens
    C. weather
    D. stealing

"Paris *covers* its costs in a number of ways."

4. The word "covers" means:

    A. gets paid back
    B. takes a loss
    C. bets
    D. counts

"Bixi has *recyclable* aluminum bikes and stations."

5. The word "recyclable" means:

    A. brand new
    B. old
    C. can be used again and again
    D. good for one time use

"Bike sharing programs are *finding their place* in transportation."

6. The phrase "finding their place" means:

    A. they have been discovered
    B. they are put in place
    C are not wanted
    D. becoming more common

WORD MAP

Directions: Follow the directions to map the word in the box below.

recycle

List 2 more words that mean the same.

List 2 more things that people recycle.

List 2 opposites or non-examples.

reprocess

Glass bottles

trash

Draw a picture below to help you remember the meaning.

Write a definition IN YOUR OWN WORDS.

LOOK WHO'S TALKING

Directions: Below are sentences from "Bike Sharing Gets Rolling." Number each paragraph. Look back in the article and re-read the paragraph in which you find the reference. Circle what you think is the best answer to each question.

1. In the second paragraph, the word "them" best refers to:

   A.   the European cities
   B.   commuters
   C.   bicycles
   D.   the people

2. In paragraph four, the word "they" refers to:

   A.   the riders
   B.   the bikes
   C.   the program
   D.   the different parts

3. In paragraph six, the word "it" refers to:

   A.   the city of Paris
   B.   the program
   C.   the riders
   D.   the stations

4. In paragraph seven, the word "its" refers to:

   A.   The riders
   B.   the actual number of bikes
   C.   the memberships
   D.   Paris

5. In paragraph eight the word "they" refers to:

   A.   the bikes
   B.   the riders
   C.   the locks
   D.   the magnetic cards

6. In paragraph ten, the word "they" refers to:

   A.   the residents
   B.   the bikes
   C.   the programs
   D.   the traffic and pollution

Name _____ Date _____

HOW'S IT ORGANIZED?

This article is organized as both **problem/solution** AND **chronological order,** *or in the time order that things happened.* The overall **problem** is how to have successful bike sharing in large cities. The **solutions** are then given in **chronological order.**

Directions: Answer these questions in the spaces at the bottom.

1. Which city first tried to start bike sharing in 1968?

2. What happened after only a month?

3. What city next tried to start bike sharing in 1994?

4. What happened to the program in that city?

5. What did Copenhagen do differently in 1995?

6. How did Paris improve the bike sharing program in 2007?

7. What did Washington, D.C., do with SmartBike DC in 2008?

8. Finally, how did Montreal improve the program in 2009?

Answers:

1.	
2.	
3.	
4.	
5.	
6.	
7.	
8.	

Name _____ Date _____

IS THAT A FACT?

Directions: Read the definitions of a <u>fact</u> and an <u>inference</u> below. Then read the paragraph that follows. At the bottom of the page, write an "F" on the blank if a sentence is a fact. Write an "I" if the sentence is an inference. Use the following definitions:

<u>Fact</u> – a statement that can be proven to be true from the article.

<u>Inference</u> – a guess as to what MIGHT be true.

Washington D.C. became the first American major city to begin a bike sharing program. The program "SmartBike" began with 120 red, three-speed bicycles at ten stations downtown. The program started with 900 members. They swiped a magnetic membership card that unlocked a bike and assigned it to them for three hours. Bike sharing programs are finding their place in transportation. Residents and visitors are saving money on gas and time for short trips. As these programs grow they create a cleaner and more peaceful environment by reducing noise and pollution. The people and the cities get healthier as a result.

_____ **1.** Bike sharing became popular very quickly.

_____ **2.** Washington, D.C., was the first American city to have bike sharing.

_____ **3.** Technology makes it less likely that the bikes will be stolen.

_____ **4.** Bike sharing can make someone healthy.

_____ **5.** The bike sharing programs help make the air cleaner.

TIME MY READ # 2

Directions: With a partner, you will see how many words you can read correctly in 45 seconds. As you read, your partner will put an "X" through any word read incorrectly. Then your partner will read while you keep score. When you have both read, trade your books or papers. Count the total number of words you read correctly. Write this score at the bottom of your page.

WORD COUNT

stations advertising exchange anti-theft Bixi electronic recyclable steal	8
residents popular unlock high-tech membership annual aluminum speed	16
vandals thieves computerized standard credit European struggling plan	24
stations advertising exchange anti-theft Bixi electronic recyclable steal	32
residents popular unlock high-tech membership annual aluminum speed	40
vandals thieves computerized standard credit European struggling plan	48
stations advertising exchange anti-theft Bixi electronic recyclable steal	56
residents popular unlock high-tech membership annual aluminum speed	64
vandals thieves computerized standard credit European struggling plan	72
stations advertising exchange anti-theft Bixi electronic recyclable steal	80

Number of words read correctly _____. Is the score higher

than it was in Time My Read #1?_____

MAKE A SPACE

Directions: Below are sentences that are missing punctuation and capitalization. First, draw slash marks (/) between the words. Then rewrite each sentence in the space below it, filling in the missing punctuation and capitalization.

> Example:
>
> cities/around/the/world/are/struggling/with/traffic
>
> Cities around the world are struggling with traffic.

1. itwaspopularbutthievesandvandalsbroughttheprogramtoanend

_____

_____

2. nowbikesharingprogramsusehightechmethodsandcomputers

_____

_____

3. washingtondcbecamethefirstamericancitywithbikesharing

_____

_____

4. astheseprogramsgrowtheycreateacleanerandhealthierenvironment

_____

_____

WORD PARTS

Directions: The prefix **trans-** means *across, beyond* or *through*. Match the following words with their definitions. Look the words up if you are not sure. Check your answers with a classmate.

1. _____ transfer

2. _____ transaction

3. _____ transport

4. _____ translate

5. _____ transform

A. a business agreement between people

B. to turn from one language into another

C. to change from one shape to another

D. to move from one place to another

E. to carry something or someone

Directions: The Greek root "kyklos" means *cycle, circle* or *wheel*. A *cycle* is a complete round of events that repeats itself. We use the root *cycle* in words like "bicycle" or "motorcycle." We also use the word *cycle* in science to explain natural events. Look up on the Internet either the **water cycle,** the **rock cycle,** or the **carbon cycle,** which is part of global warming. Draw a picture of this cycle on the circle below.

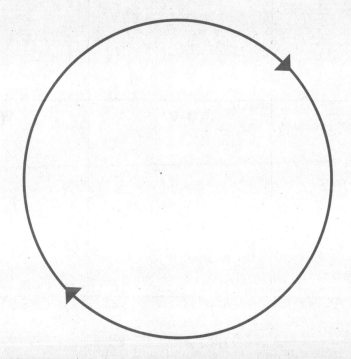

SUMMARIZING ABC's

Directions: Now that you've read the article about bike sharing in cities, see how many words you can fill in the boxes below.

A–C	D–F	G–I
J–L	M–O	P–R
S–T	U–V	W–Z

SENTENCE SUMMARIES

Directions: Below are 4 key words from the article "Bike Sharing Gets Rolling." Your job is to summarize, or restate, what you've learned in this article by using these 4 words or phrases in two sentences. Then, as a challenge, try to use all 4 words or phrases in one sentence to restate the article.

FOUR KEY WORDS OR PHRASES

traffic   theft
bicycles   payment

Sentence Summaries:

1. _____

_____

2. _____

_____

Challenge Summary (All 4 words or phrases in one sentence!)

1. _____

_____

_____

TAKE A STAND

Directions: People often have different feelings, or opinions, about the same thing. A "debate" is when people argue their different ideas. A good, persuasive argument has the following:

Facts – statements that can be proven to be true.

Statistics – research from a scientific study that uses numbers.

Examples – stories from the world that support an opinion.

You and a partner are going to debate two of your other classmates. The topic you are going to debate is the following:

Cities should not allow cars in their downtown areas.

Decide whether you agree or disagree with this statement. Then answer these questions in order to win your debate.

1. What are your 2 strongest points to persuade the other side?
(You can do Internet research to include facts, statistics, and examples.)

A. _____

B. _____

2. What will the other side say to argue against point A?

_____

_____

3. What will the other side say to argue against point B?

_____

_____

4. What will you say to prove the other side's arguments are wrong?

_____

_____

ASSESSMENT

Comprehension: Answer the questions about the passage below.

Bike sharing began in the Netherlands. Programs at first asked too little of the riders, but now there are new high-tech methods to keep track of the bikes. Computerized programs now can text message a rider and the program knows who is riding the bike. Washington D.C. became the first American city to have a bike sharing program.

These programs are finding their place in transportation. Residents and visitors are saving money and time on short trips. The exercise they get makes the riders and the cities healthier, and keeps the environment cleaner.

1. Why might it be a good idea to have a bike sharing program?

_____

_____

2. What was needed to prevent abuse and theft of the bikes?

_____

_____

3. What was the author's purpose for writing this article about bikes?

_____

_____

Fluency: The words in the two sentences are all connected. The sentences are also missing punctuation and capitalization. Draw slash marks (/) between the words. Then rewrite the sentence, filling in the punctuation and capitalization.

1. pariscoversitscostsinanumberofways

_____

_____

2. itbeganwithtenthousandbikesandwasverysuccessfulfromthestart

_____

_____

Name _____ Date _____

Fluency: Read the three sentences below. Imagine where you would pause within each sentence as you read it aloud. Draw a slash (/) mark between the phrases where you would pause. The first slash is done.

3. Riders / use credit cards to pay about $1.50 a day to ride the bikes.

4. There are few problems with theft because the program knows who is riding the bikes.

5. The electronic system for locking and paying for bikes at the stations runs on solar power.

Vocabulary: Based on what you have learned in this lesson, match the following words with their definitions. Write the letter of the definition on the blank in front of the word it defines.

1. _____ transform   **A.** people who live in an area

2. _____ residents   **B.** a business agreement between people

3. _____ recycle   **C.** to change from one shape to another

4. _____ transport   **D.** to need; must have

5. _____ translate   **E.** to carry something or someone

6. _____ theft   **F.** to turn from one language into another

7. _____ transaction   **G.** gets paid back

8. _____ covers   **H.** reuse or reprocess

9. _____ transfer   **I.** stolen

10. _____ require   **J.** to move something or someone from one place to another

Name _____ Date _____

ANTICIPATION GUIDE

Directions: <u>Before</u> you read the article "The Sounds of Jazz Are in the Air," read the statements below. If you agree with a statement, put a check on the line. Otherwise, leave it blank.

_____ **1.** Outdoor jazz festivals have been around since 1930.

_____ **2.** There are many different styles of jazz music.

_____ **3.** Learning about jazz is an essential part of any American's education.

Once you have checked the statements above, tell why you agreed or disagreed with each statement in the section below.

1. _____

_____

2. _____

_____

3. _____

_____

In the box below, draw a picture of what you think this article is about.

What's Happening
IN CALIFORNIA?

By Lawrence Gable
© 2010 What's Happening Publications

Subject: Art

The Sounds of Jazz Are in the Air

Monterey lies at the southern end of the Monterey Bay. Tourists go there to enjoy its historic buildings, its aquarium and the great natural beauty. For more than 50 years, though, they also have been going to the Monterey County Fairgrounds for music. Every September the Monterey Jazz Festival offers fans three nights and two days of jazz.

Monterey's is the longest-running jazz festival in the world. It began in 1958 and has become America's greatest jazz event. Now more than 50 performances take place indoors and outdoors on nine stages.

The festival's founder dreamt of a weekend of jazz with the world's best musicians. At that time jazz musicians performed mostly in small nightclubs. Playing outside among beautiful oak trees was exceptional. Among the great musicians at the 1958 festival were Louis Armstrong, Sonny Rollins, Billie Holiday and Dave Brubeck.

Mr. Brubeck has a long history with the festival. He performed for Monterey's city council when it was deciding whether to approve the festival. Since then he has performed at Monterey more than a dozen times. He is still composing, recording and touring.

Over the years the Monterey Jazz Festival has offered a variety of styles. Performers have played Dixieland, bebop, swing, big band, rock, salsa and blues. Every year the line-up includes jazz legends and current stars. Real fans also enjoy discovering little-known performers who play on the festival's small stages.

The festival also promotes jazz through education. Its programs give students in Monterey County instruments, classes and opportunities to perform. During the school year professional musicians work with students in classrooms. Every summer it also hosts a two-week jazz camp. Finally, its Next Generation Festival builds the future of jazz by inviting top students from around the world.

The festival also has some special projects. For its 50th anniversary it published a book that tells about its history and includes photos and posters. The festival also has begun its own record label for historic recordings. Also, the festival now has a Digital Music Education Project. At this Web site jazz musicians give tips and talk about the artists who influenced them.

In 1958 about 7,000 fans saw music from one stage. Now more than 40,000 people enjoy the music, workshops, exhibits and food. Together they celebrate America's gift to music, jazz.

REACTION GUIDE

Directions: <u>Now that you have read</u> "The Sounds of Jazz Are in the Air," reread the statements below. Then think about how the author would feel about these statements. If you think the author would agree, put a check on the line before the number. Then, below the statement, copy the words, phrases, or sentences in the article that tell you the author's real views.

_____ **1.** Outdoor jazz festivals have been around since 1930.

Article notes: _____

_____

_____

_____ **2.** There are many different styles of jazz music.

Article notes: _____

_____

_____

_____ **3.** Learning about jazz is an essential part of any American's education.

Article notes: _____

_____

_____

WORDSTORM

Directions: It's good to know more than just the dictionary definition of a word. A wordstorm lets you write down information that helps you understand what a word means, how it's related to other words, and how to use it in different ways.

What is the word?

festival
_____

Copy the sentence from the text in which the word is used:

_____

_____

What are some other words or phrases that mean the same thing?

_____

What are three examples of a festival?

1. _____ 2. _____ 3. _____

Name three people who would likely use this word other than

teachers.

1. _____ 2. _____ 3. _____

Draw a picture that reminds you of the word "festival" below:

TIME MY READ # 1

Directions: With a partner, you will see how many words you can read correctly in 45 seconds. As you read, your partner will put an "X" through any word read incorrectly. Then your partner will read while you keep score. When you have both read, trade your books or papers. Count the total number of words you read correctly. Write this score at the bottom of your page.

WORD COUNT

Monterey Bay tourists music anniversary jazz festival performances	8
stages nightclubs exceptional Louis Armstrong composing recording touring	16
bebop Dixieland discovering blues programs opportunities influenced musicians	24
Monterey Bay tourists music anniversary jazz festival performances	32
stages nightclubs exceptional Louis Armstrong composing recording touring	40
bebop Dixieland discovering blues programs opportunities influenced musicians	48
Monterey Bay tourists music anniversary jazz festival performances	56
stages nightclubs exceptional Louis Armstrong composing recording touring	64
bebop Dixieland discovering blues programs opportunities influenced musicians	72
Monterey Bay tourists music anniversary jazz festival performances	80

Number of words read correctly _____.

ECHO READING

Directions: When you read, you should make breaks between groups of words. As the teacher reads each phrase, repeat aloud what was read and underline that phrase. Then you will read the whole sentence aloud together. The first sentence has been underlined for you.

Monterey lies at the southern end of the Monterey Bay.
Tourists go there to enjoy its historic buildings, its aquarium and
the great natural beauty. For more than 50 years, though, they
also have been going to the Monterey County Fairgrounds for
music. Every September the Monterey Jazz Festival offers fans
three nights and two days of jazz.

Monterey's is the longest-running jazz festival in the world. It
began in 1958 and has become America's greatest jazz event.
Now more than 50 performances take place indoors and
outdoors on nine stages.

The festival's founder dreamt of a weekend with the world's
best musicians. At that time most jazz musicians performed in
small nightclubs. Playing outside among the giant oak trees was
exceptional.

GET A CONTEXT CLUE

Directions: Below are sentences from "The Sounds of Jazz Are in the Air." Read the sentence. Look back in the article and read the paragraph the sentence is in. Circle what you think is the best answer to each question

"Tourists go there to enjoy its *historic* buildings, its aquarium, and its great natural beauty."

1. The word "historic" means:

A. beautiful
B. strange
C. large
D. old and important

"Monterey's is the *longest-running* jazz festival in the world."

2. The phrase "longest-running" means:

A. able to run a great distance
B. been around for a long time
C. a name for a marathon
D. fairly new

"Playing outside among beautiful oak trees was *exceptional*."

3. The word "exceptional" means:

A. nice
B. outstanding
C. scary
D. weird

"Every year the line-up includes jazz *legends* and current stars."

4. The word "legends" means:

A. storytellers
B. famous people
C. children
D. gamblers

"Real *fans* also enjoy discovering performers who play on the festival's small stages."

5. The word "fans" means:

A. machines to cool you
B. visitors
C. admirers
D. tourists

"At this Web site jazz musicians give tips and talk about the artists who *influenced* them."

6. The term "influenced" means:

A. made them angry
B. had a big impact on them
C. paid them
D. talked to them

WORD CHOICE

Directions: As you read this piece, you will find blanks for missing words. Three words are listed after the blank. One of these is correct. <u>Read the rest of the sentence past the blank to figure out which is the correct word</u>. Write it in the blank.

Monterey lies at the southern end of the Monterey Bay.

Tourists _____ (goes, gone, go) there to enjoy

_____ (it's, its, if) historic buildings, aquarium and the great

natural beauty. Every September, though, they go to the

Monterey County Fairgrounds for three _____ (years,

nights, hours) and two days of music. The year 2007 was the

50ᵗʰ _____ (anniversary, time, show) of the Monterey

Jazz Festival.

Monterey's is the longest-running jazz festival in the world. It

_____ (begins, began, beginning) in 1958 and

_____ (has, was, be) become America's greatest jazz event.

Each year more than 50 performances take place indoors and

outdoors on nine stages.

Every summer the festival _____ (hosting, hosts, host) a

summer jazz camp for two weeks. There a performance

_____ (calls, calling, called) the Next Generation Festival

_____ (builds, built, building) the festival's and the

music's future.

Name _____ Date _____

LOOK WHO'S TALKING

Directions: Below are sentences from "The Sounds of Jazz Are in the Air." Number each paragraph. Look back in the article and re-read the paragraph in which you find the reference. Circle what you think is the best answer to each question.

1. In the first paragraph, the word "there" best refers to:

A. the festival
B. the city of Monterey
C. the month of the festival
D. the buildings in Monterey

2. In paragraph two, the word "it" refers to:

A. the bay
B. the jazz
C. the festival
D. the city of Monterey

3. In paragraph four, the word "he" refers to:

A. Dave Brubeck
B. Sonny Rollins
C. Billie Holiday
D. Louis Armstrong

4. In paragraph five, the word "who" refers to:

A. new artists
B. artists who are not yet famous
C. artists who are not that good
D. artists who don't know much about music

5. In paragraph six, the word "its" refers to:

A. the festival
B. the jazz camp
C. the city of Monterey
D. the students from around the world

6. In paragraph eight the word "they" refers to:

A. the musicians
B. the festival
C. the 40,000 people
D. the 7,000 fans

NOTE MAKING

Directions: Read the key **bold** words on the left side of the chart below. Then add notes that answer the question in parentheses under the key word.

Jazz Festival

(Where?)

Festival started

(When?)

Musicians

(Who?)

Education

(How?)

Digital Project

(Why?)

Name _____ Date _____

IS THAT A FACT?

Directions: Read the definitions of a <u>fact</u> and an <u>inference</u> below. Then read the paragraph that follows. At the bottom of the page, write an "F" on the blank if a sentence is a fact or an "I" if it is an inference. Use the following definitions:

<u>Fact</u> – a statement that can be proven to be true from the article.

<u>Inference</u> – a guess as to what MIGHT be true.

   The festival promotes jazz through education. Its programs give students in the Monterey County instruments, classes and opportunities to perform. During the school year professional musicians work with students in classrooms. Every summer it also hosts a two-week jazz camp. Finally, its Next Generation Festival builds the future of jazz by inviting top students from around the world. In 1958 about 7,000 fans saw music from one stage. Now more than 40,000 people enjoy the music, workshops, exhibits and food.

_____ **1.** The Monterey Jazz Festival is very well known.

_____ **2.** The musicians have a strong interest in keeping their music alive.

_____ **3.** Around forty thousand people attend the festival.

_____ **4.** The attractions at the festival have expanded greatly.

_____ **5.** Students living near Monterey have a great opportunity to learn jazz.

_____ **6.** The festival began in 1958.

TIME MY READ # 2

Directions: With a partner, you will see how many words you can read correctly in 45 seconds. As you read, your partner will put an "X" through any word read incorrectly. Then your partner will read while you keep score. When you have both read, trade your books or papers. Count the total number of words you read correctly. Write this score at the bottom of your page.

WORD COUNT

Monterey Bay tourists music anniversary jazz festival performances	8
stages nightclubs exceptional Louis Armstrong composing recording touring	16
bebop Dixieland discovering blues programs opportunities influenced musicians	24
Monterey Bay tourists music anniversary jazz festival performances	32
stages nightclubs exceptional Louis Armstrong composing recording touring	40
bebop Dixieland discovering blues programs opportunities influenced musicians	48
Monterey Bay tourists music anniversary jazz festival performances	56
stages nightclubs exceptional Louis Armstrong composing recording touring	64
bebop Dixieland discovering blues programs opportunities influenced musicians	72
Monterey Bay tourists music anniversary jazz festival performances	80

Number of words read correctly _____. Is the score higher

than it was in Time My Read #1?_____

"The Sounds of Jazz Are in the Air"

MAKE A SPACE

Directions: Below are sentences that are missing punctuation and capitalization. First, draw slash marks (/) between the words. Then rewrite each sentence in the space below it, filling in the missing punctuation and capitalization.

Example:

monterey/lies/at/the/southern/end/of/the/monterey/bay

Monterey lies at the southern end of the Monterey Bay.

1. overtheyearsthemontereyjazzfestivalhasofferedavarietyofstyles

_____

_____

2. thefestivalalsopromotesjazzthrougheducation

_____

_____

3. everysummeritalsohostsatwoweekjazzcamp

_____

_____

4. thefestivalalsohasbegunitsownrecordlabelforhistoricrecordings

_____

_____

Name _____ Date _____

Directions: A suffix is added to the end of a base word to change how it's used in a sentence. Look at the sentence below.

*Tourists go there to enjoy its **historic** buildings.*

Adding the suffix **–ic** turns the **noun** "history" into an **adjective** describing buildings as "historic." (Sometimes the spelling of the base word changes slightly.) The suffix **–ic** means *having the characteristics of.* Write a definition of the words below. Look up any unknown words.

1. electronic – _____

2. poetic – _____

3. tragic – _____

4. moronic – _____

5. mechanic – _____

6. volcanic – _____

7. futuristic – _____

8. photographic – _____

9. diplomatic – _____

10. comedic – _____

Directions: Draw pictures to show the meanings of 2 of these words.

JAZZ CROSSWORD PUZZLE

Directions: Complete the crossword puzzle.

Across

1 something very sad

7 outstanding; amazing

8 something that makes people laugh

10 a person who is known as one of the best in what he or she does

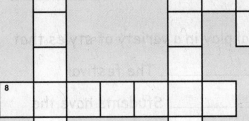

Down

2 to have an impact on; to affect something or someone

3 something very stupid

4 lasting a long time

5 something old and important

6 an event where people gather to celebrate something

9 a follower or admirer of something or someone

Word List

LONG-RUNNING	EXCEPTIONAL	FAN	HISTORIC	TRAGIC
MORONIC	LEGEND	COMEDIC	INFLUENCE	FESTIVAL

WRITING FRAME

Directions: Below is a writing frame. Use your knowledge and information from the article to complete the frame below.

Tourists go to the Monterey County Fairgrounds every September in order to be a part of the three nights and two days of _____. For more than 50 years, though, they also have been going to the _____ for music. Every September the Monterey Jazz Festival offers fans _____. Some of the musicians that performed at the first Monterey Jazz Festival in 1958 included _____.

The performers at the festival play in a variety of styles that include _____. The festival promotes jazz through _____. Students have the opportunity to work with _____. For its 50th anniversary it published a book that _____. The festival also has begun its own _____. Now more than 40,000 people gather to celebrate America's gift to music, _____.

TAKE A STAND

Directions: People often have different feelings, or opinions, about the same thing. A "debate" is when people argue their different ideas. A good, persuasive argument has the following:

Facts – statements that can be proven to be true.

Statistics – research from a scientific study that uses numbers.

Examples – stories from the world that support an opinion.

You and a partner are going to debate two of your other classmates. The topic you are going to debate is the following:

Learning about jazz is an essential part of any American's education.

Decide whether you agree or disagree with this statement. Then answer these questions in order to win your debate.

1. What are your 2 strongest points to persuade the other side?
(You can do Internet research to include facts, statistics, and examples.)

A. _____

B. _____

2. What will the other side say to argue against point A?

_____

_____

3. What will the other side say to argue against point B?

_____

_____

4. What will you say to prove the other side's arguments are wrong?

_____

_____

ASSESSMENT

Comprehension: Answer the questions about the passage below.

Monterey's is the longest-running jazz festival in the world. It began in 1958 and has become America's greatest jazz event. Over fifty performances take place indoors and outdoors on nine small stages. Over the years the festival has offered a variety of artistic styles. Performers have played Dixieland, bebop, swing, big band, rock, salsa and blues. Recent line-ups have included Sonny Rollins, Dave Brubeck, Diana Krall, and Los Lobos. Fans also enjoy discovering little-known performers who play on the festival's small stages.

1. Why might the Monterey Jazz Festival be so popular?

_____

_____

2. What are the types of music that a person can hear there?

_____

_____

3. What was the author's purpose for writing about the festival?

_____

_____

Fluency: The words in the two sentences are all connected. The sentences are also missing punctuation and capitalization. Draw slash marks (/) between the words. Then rewrite the sentence, filling in the punctuation and capitalization.

1. alsothefestivalnowhasadigitalmusiceducationproject

_____

_____

2. overtheyearsthemontereyjazzfestivalhasofferedavarietyofstyles

_____

_____

Name _____ Date _____

ASSESSMENT

Fluency: Read the three sentences below. Imagine where you would pause within each sentence as you read it aloud. Draw a slash (/) mark between the phrases where you would pause. The first slash is done.

3. Monterey's / is the longest running jazz festival in the world.

4. In 1958 about 7,000 fans saw music from one stage.

5. At this Web site jazz musicians give tips and talk about the artists who influenced them.

Vocabulary: Based on what you have learned in this lesson, match the following words with their definitions. Write the letter of the definition on the blank in front of the word it defines.

1. _____ tragic   **A.** very funny

2. _____ fan   **B.** very sad

3. _____ historic   **C.** to have an impact or effect on

4. _____ long-running   **D.** outstanding; amazing

5. _____ festival   **E.** lasting a long time

6. _____ moronic   **F.** someone well-known in his or her field

7. _____ legend   **G.** a follower or admirer

8. _____ comedic   **H.** an event where people celebrate

9. _____ influence   **I.** very stupid

10. _____ exceptional   **J.** old and important

Name _____ Date _____

ANTICIPATION GUIDE

Directions: <u>Before</u> you read the article "New Jersey Abolishes the Death Penalty," read the statements below. If you agree with a statement, put a check on the line. Otherwise, leave it blank.

_____ **1.** Putting criminals to death keeps others from murdering.

_____ **2.** Sometimes innocent people in jail are put to death.

_____ **3.** The death penalty is a fair punishment.

Once you have checked the statements above, tell why you agreed or disagreed with each statement in the section below.

1. _____

_____

2. _____

_____

3. _____

_____

In the box below, draw a picture of what you think this article is about.

"New Jersey Abolishes the Death Penalty"

What's Happening
IN THE USA?

By Lawrence Gable
© *2010 What's Happening Publications*

Subject: Human Rights

Each state in the U.S. can decide whether it has the death penalty. New Jersey has had it, but it has not executed anyone since 1963. In December 2007 its legislature voted to abolish the death penalty. It became the first state in forty years to do that.

In 2006 New Jersey formed a Death Penalty Study Commission. The commission's 13 members studied the effects of the death penalty in their state. Then in November 2006 they recommended the abolition of the death penalty.

The commissioners looked into a number of questions. One was whether the death penalty lowers murder rates. It was impossible for them to find a clear answer. On the one hand, national rates had fallen since 1976 when the U.S. Supreme Court allowed the death penalty. On the other hand, in 2005 murder rates were higher in states that have the death penalty. Experts also say that many things affect murder rates, including employment rates and gun laws.

The commission also studied costs. It found that the death penalty was a more expensive sentence than life in prison. In 2006 the state spent $84,474 housing each person on death row. However, among other prisoners it spent only $32,400 per prisoner. The state also spent millions fighting the many legal appeals that came after a death sentence.

New Jersey's commission investigated whether the death penalty serves the victims' families. Because the punishment is extreme, the courts take extra time with the cases. The legal appeals delay the execution. Commissioners felt that this extends the families' suffering.

NEW JERSEY ABOLISHES THE DEATH PENALTY

Finally, it looked at the risk of executing an innocent person. Sometimes crime labs or witnesses make mistakes. Even worse, sometimes police lie or lawyers hide information. Years after a trial DNA tests sometimes prove someone's innocence. Since 1973, 124 innocent people on death rows in the U.S. had gone free. The commission recommended sentences of life in prison.

Americans' opinions about the death penalty change. A poll in 2006 showed that change. When they had the choice, people preferred a life sentence without parole (48 percent) to the death penalty (47 percent).

Most states execute prisoners by lethal injection. The method uses three chemicals and takes only a few minutes. However, some executioners have injected the chemicals incorrectly, so the deaths have been long and painful. After one such case in Florida in 2006 the governor suspended executions.

A case before the U.S. Supreme Court in 2008 caused all states to stop executions. Two prisoners in Kentucky felt that lethal injection violates U. S. law, which bans "cruel and unusual punishment." The case was important because Americans do not approve of old methods like electric chairs, gas chambers and firing squads. The Court, however, ruled in favor of lethal injections.

Some states have stopped executions, but not abolished them. Those decisions came from courts or governors. New Jersey was different because the change came from legislators. They decided that the death penalty does not serve the people well, so they made their state the 14th in the nation without it.

Name _____ Date _____

Directions: <u>Now that you have read</u> "New Jersey Abolishes the Death Penalty," reread the statements below. Then think about how the author would feel about these statements. If you think the author would agree, put a check on the line before the number. Then, below the statement, copy the words, phrases, or sentences in the article that tell you the author's real views.

_____ **1.** Putting criminals to death keeps others from murdering.

Article notes: _____

_____

_____

_____ **2.** Sometimes innocent people in jail are put to death.

Article notes: _____

_____

_____

_____ **3.** The death penalty is a fair punishment.

Article notes: _____

_____

_____

PREDICTING ABC's

Directions: The article you are going to read is about "executions." See how many boxes you can fill in below with words about putting people to death for a crime they have committed. For example, put the word "prison" in the P–R box. Try to put at least one word in every box.

A–C	D–F	G–I
J–L	M–O	P–R
S–T	U–V	W–Z

TIME MY READ # 1

Directions: With a partner, you will see how many words you can read correctly in 45 seconds. As you read, your partner will put an "X" through any word read incorrectly. Then your partner will read while you keep score. When you have both read, trade your books or papers. Count the total number of words you read correctly. Write this score at the bottom of your page.

WORD COUNT

penalty execution abolition legislators sentence expensive approve states	8
preferred opinions commission chemicals national appeals chambers court	16
witnesses legislature innocent parole whether prison housing unusual	24
penalty execution abolition legislators sentence expensive approve states	32
preferred opinions commission chemicals national appeals chambers court	40
witnesses legislature innocent parole whether prison housing unusual	48
penalty execution abolition legislators sentence expensive approve states	56
preferred opinions commission chemicals national appeals chambers court	64
witnesses legislature innocent parole whether prison housing unusual	72
penalty execution abolition legislators sentence expensive approve states	80

Number of words read correctly _____.

ECHO READING

Directions: Your teacher will read aloud the text below. Listen carefully. Draw lines under the words he or she groups together. The first sentence has been done for you.

The commissioners looked into a number of questions. One question was whether the death penalty lowers murder rates. It was impossible for them to find a clear answer. On the one hand, national rates have fallen since 1976 when the U. S. Supreme Court allowed the death penalty. On the other hand, in 2005 murder rates were higher in states that have the death penalty. Experts say that many things affect murder rates, including employment rates and gun laws.

The commission also studied costs. It found that the death penalty was a much more expensive sentence than life in prison. In 2006 the state spent $84,474 housing each person on death row. However, among other prisoners it spent only $32,000 per prisoner.

GET A CONTEXT CLUE

Directions: Below are sentences from "New Jersey Abolishes the Death Penalty." Read the sentence. Look back in the article and read the paragraph the sentence is in. Circle what you think is the best answer to each question.

"In 2006 New Jersey formed a Death Penalty Study *Commission*."

1. The word "commission" means:

   A. test
   B. group
   C. session
   D. idea

"The legal appeals *delay* the execution."

2. The word "delay" means:

   A. strengthen
   B. forbid
   C. quicken
   D. put off for another time

"Most states execute prisoners through lethal injections."

3. The word "lethal" means:

   A. causing death
   B. preserving life
   C. accusation
   D. the crime

"Finally, it looked at the *risk* of executing an innocent person."

4. The word "risk" means:

   A. danger
   B. reason
   C. method or technique
   D. fairness

"A *poll* in 2006 showed that change."

5. The word "poll" means:

   A. discussion
   B. new law
   C. survey
   D. newspaper

"The Court, however, ruled *in favor of* lethal injections."

6. The phrase "in favor of" means:

   A. for; in support of
   B. in reaction to
   C. about
   D. against

WORD MAP

Directions: Follow the directions to map the word in the box below.

> **abolish**

List 2 more words
that mean the same.

List 2 more examples.

List 2 opposites or
non-examples.

| ban | | a rule that stops student snacks | | continue |

Draw a picture below to help
you remember the meaning.

Write a definition IN
YOUR OWN WORDS.

LOOK WHO'S TALKING

Directions: Below are sentences from "New Jersey Abolishes the Death Penalty." Number each paragraph. Look back in the article and re-read the paragraph in which you find the reference. Circle what you think is the best answer to each question.

1. In the first paragraph, the word "it" appears multiple times and best refers to:

    A.   the death penalty
    B.   the U.S.
    C.   New Jersey
    D.   the legislature

2. In paragraph two, the word "their" refers to:

    A.   the commission
    B.   the legislature
    C.   the state of New Jersey
    D.   the U.S.

3. In paragraph four, the word "it" refers to:

    A.   the state
    B.   the commission
    C.   the legislature
    D.   the U.S.

4. In paragraph eight, the word "method" refers to:

    A.   the lethal injection
    B.   the chemicals
    C.   the means of injecting
    D.   life sentence without parole

5. In paragraph ten the sentence "Some states have stopped executions but have not abolished them" means:

    A.   there are no more executions
    B.   executions are continuing
    C.   no more lethal injections
    D.   the executions are still allowed

6. In paragraph ten, the word "their" refers to:

    A.   the people of New Jersey
    B.   the legislature
    C.   the prisons
    D.   the nation

HOW'S IT ORGANIZED?

This article is organized in a compare and contrast form. This means some things are *compared that are alike or similar* and some are *contrasted, or shown how they are different.*

Directions: Answer these questions in the spaces at the bottom.

1. What did New Jersey do in 2007 that contrasted with all other states?

2. What are 2 things the commission compared about executions?

3. How do the costs of executions and life in prison compare?

4. In 2006, how did Americans' opinions about executions compare with their opinions about life in prison?

5. What did the Supreme Court rule about lethal injections that contrasted with "cruel and unusual punishment"?

6. How did New Jersey's decision contrast with the way other states have halted executions?

Answers:

1.	
2.	
3.	
4.	
5.	
6.	

IS THAT A FACT?

Directions: Read the definitions of a <u>fact</u> and an <u>inference</u> below. Then read the paragraph that follows. At the bottom of the page, write an "F" on the blank if a sentence is a fact. Write an "I" if the sentence is an inference. Use the following definitions:

<u>Fact</u> – a statement that can be proven to be true from the article.

<u>Inference</u> – a guess as to what MIGHT be true.

"Americans' opinions about the death penalty are changing. A poll in 2006 showed that change. When they had the choice, people preferred a life sentence without parole (48 percent) to the death penalty (47 percent). Most states execute prisoners by lethal injection. This method uses three chemicals and only takes a few minutes. However, some executioners have injected the chemicals incorrectly, so the deaths were long and painful."

_____ **1.** Americans are divided in their opinions about the death penalty.

_____ **2.** The way prisoners are executed has some problems.

_____ **3.** Use of chemicals for executions is efficient most of the time.

_____ **4.** Most states use the method of lethal injection.

_____ **5.** Most states no longer use the electric chair for executions.

TIME MY READ # 2

Directions: With a partner, you will see how many words you can read correctly in 45 seconds. As you read, your partner will put an "X" through any word read incorrectly. Then your partner will read while you keep score. When you have both read, trade your books or papers. Count the total number of words you read correctly. Write this score at the bottom of your page.

WORD COUNT

penalty execution abolition legislators sentence expensive approve states	8
preferred opinions commission chemicals national appeals chambers court	16
witnesses legislature innocent parole whether prison housing unusual	24
penalty execution abolition legislators sentence expensive approve states	32
preferred opinions commission chemicals national appeals chambers court	40
witnesses legislature innocent parole whether prison housing unusual	48
penalty execution abolition legislators sentence expensive approve states	56
preferred opinions commission chemicals national appeals chambers court	64
witnesses legislature innocent parole whether prison housing unusual	72
penalty execution abolition legislators sentence expensive approve states	80

Number of words read correctly _____. Is the score higher

than it was in Time My Read #1?_____

MAKE A SPACE

Directions: Below are sentences that are missing punctuation and capitalization. First, draw slash marks (/) between the words. Then rewrite each sentence in the space below it, filling in the missing punctuation and capitalization.

Example:

americans/opinions/are/changing/about/the/death/penalty

Americans' opinions are changing about the death penalty.

1. moststatesexecuteprisonersbylethalinjection

_____

_____

2. becausethepunishmentisextremecourtstakemoretimewiththecase

_____

_____

3. americansdonotapproveoftheoldmethodslikeelectricchairsorgaschambers

_____

_____

4. murderrateswerehigherinstatesthathadthedeathpenalty

_____

_____

WORD PARTS

Directions: A suffix is added to the end of a base word to change how it's used in a sentence. Suffixes do this in many ways. The suffix **–ing** is most often used as a **verb** showing action. For example, "Juan is *flying* to Mexico today." "Flying" is called a present participle.

The suffix **–ing** can also be added to the end of a **verb** to make a **noun**, or thing. For example, by adding **–ing** to the **verb** "build," you get the **noun** "building." Sometimes a word ending in **–ing** acts like an **adjective** by describing something. For example, "My mother is at her *sewing* machine." The word "sewing" tells us what kind of machine.

The following sentences come from the article on the death penalty. Write a definition of the words having an **–ing** suffix. You can look in a dictionary, on the Internet, or ask a partner if you don't know.

1. "Experts also say that many things affect murder rates, **including** employment rates and gun laws."

Definition:_____

2. "In 2006 the state spent $84,474 **housing** each person on death row."

Definition:_____

3. "Commissioners felt that this extends the families' **suffering**."

Definition:_____

4. "Finally, it looked at the risk of **executing** an innocent person."

Definition:_____

5. "The case was important because Americans do not approve of old methods like electric chairs, gas chambers, and **firing** squads."

Definition:_____

SUMMARIZING ABC's

Directions: Now that you've read the article on the death penalty, see how many words you can fill in the boxes below.

A–C	D–F	G–I
J–L	**M–O**	**P–R**
S–T	**U–V**	**W–Z**

"New Jersey Abolishes the Death Penalty"

Name _____ Date _____

SENTENCE SUMMARIES

Directions: Below are 4 key words from the article "New Jersey Abolishes the Death Penalty." Your job is to summarize, or restate, what you've learned in this article by using these 4 words or phrases in two sentences. Then, as a challenge, try to use all 4 words or phrases in one sentence to restate the article.

FOUR KEY WORDS OR PHRASES

death penalty   U.S. Supreme Court
cruel and unusual punishment   abolish

Sentence Summaries:

1. _____

_____

2. _____

_____

Challenge Summary (All 4 words or phrases in one sentence!)

1. _____

_____

_____

TAKE A STAND

Directions: People often have different feelings, or opinions, about the same thing. A "debate" is when people argue their different ideas. A good, persuasive argument has the following:

Facts – statements that can be proven to be true.

Statistics – research from a scientific study that uses numbers.

Examples – stories from the world that support an opinion.

You and a partner are going to debate two of your other classmates. The topic you are going to debate is the following:

The death penalty is a fair punishment.

Decide whether you agree or disagree with this statement. Then answer these questions in order to win your debate.

1. What are your 2 strongest points to persuade the other side?
(You can do Internet research to include facts, statistics, and examples.)

A. _____

B. _____

2. What will the other side say to argue against point A?

_____

_____

3. What will the other side say to argue against point B?

_____

_____

4. What will you say to prove the other side's arguments are wrong?

_____

_____

ASSESSMENT

Comprehension: Answer the questions about the passage below.

Sometimes crime labs or witnesses make mistakes. Even worse, sometimes police lie or lawyers hide information. Americans' opinions about the death penalty are divided. Some states have stopped executions, but not abolished them. Those decisions came from courts or governors. New Jersey is different because the change came from legislators. They decided that the death penalty does not serve the people well, so they made their state the 14th in the nation without it.

1. What makes New Jersey's actions different?

_____

_____

2. Why would people object to the death penalty?

_____

_____

3. What do you think the author is saying by writing this article?

_____

_____

Fluency: The words in the two sentences are all connected. The sentences are also missing punctuation and capitalization. Draw slash marks (/) between the words. Then rewrite the sentence, filling in the punctuation and capitalization.

1. americansopinionsaboutthedeathpenaltychange

_____

_____

2. acasebeforetheussupremecourtin2008causedallstatestostopexecutions

_____

_____

Name _____ Date _____

Fluency: Read the three sentences below. Imagine where you would pause within each sentence as you read it aloud. Draw a slash (/) mark between the phrases where you would pause. The first slash is done.

3. The commissioners / looked into a number of questions.

4. Each state in the U.S. can decide whether or not it has a death penalty.

5. Finally, it looked at the risk of executing an innocent person.

Vocabulary: Based on what you have learned in this lesson, match the following words with their definitions. Write the letter of the definition on the blank in front of the word it defines.

1. _____ housing   **A.** hurting

2. _____ abolish   **B.** providing a place to live

3. _____ delay   **C.** a group organized to do something

4. _____ in favor of   **D.** putting someone to death

5. _____ executing   **E.** survey

6. _____ lethal   **F.** to stop permanently

7. _____ poll   **G.** danger

8. _____ suffering   **H.** causing death

9. _____ commission   **I.** to put off for another time

10. _____ risk   **J.** for; in support of

Name _____ Date _____

ANTICIPATION GUIDE

Directions: <u>Before</u> you read the article "Families of Missing Persons Get Help," read the statements below. If you agree with a statement, put a check on the line. Otherwise, leave it blank.

_____ **1.** Many people besides soldiers are lost in wars.

_____ **2.** Losing a relative is sad but not much of a practical problem.

_____ **3.** It is okay to kill civilians during a war if it helps end the conflict sooner.

Once you have checked the statements above, tell why you agreed or disagreed with each statement in the section below.

1. _____

_____

2. _____

_____

3. _____

_____

In the box below, draw a picture of what you think this article is about.

What's Happening
IN THE WORLD?

By Lawrence Gable
© 2010 What's Happening Publications

Subject: Global Issues

Families of Missing Persons Get Help

When countries are at war, many soldiers and civilians go missing. This happened to hundreds of thousands of people during the Iran-Iraq War (1980–88). Many of their families still do not know what happened to their relatives. In 2008 Iran and Iraq signed an agreement to work with the Red Cross to find those missing persons.

Since 1863 the International Committee of the Red Cross (ICRC) has helped victims of war all over the world. In fact, humanitarian law gives the ICRC the power to protect the dignity of the victims of war. That includes identifying missing persons.

The ICRC works with countries to get information about missing persons. They include soldiers who may have died or become prisoners. They also include large numbers of civilians who have become targets in modern warfare. Civilians die in attacks on their towns and villages. Many flee to other places for safety, even to a neighboring country. Too often small children become separated from their families.

Identifying the dead takes time. Because of the many wars around the world, scientists have become more and more exact. They take DNA or blood samples from family members in order to help identify a body.

The ICRC gathers all the information that it can about missing persons. It uses records from governments and from Red Cross workers who visit prisons, hospitals and mortuaries. When it identifies someone, it tries to reach the family. It sends information out through its own Web site, radio and printed messages. If it can, it contacts families directly. When things go well, it reunites families.

Relatives suffer emotional pain when they do not know the fate of a loved one. They worry that the relative may be dead and lying in an unmarked grave. They also worry that the relative might be alive, but suffering horribly in a prison or hospital. In either case, they continue to hope that the relative will return.

Having a missing relative also affects practical parts of daily life. It delays the inheritance of land, property and money. It also prevents a spouse from remarrying and creating a new life. In some cultures the grown children cannot marry without the permission of a parent who is missing.

The ICRC played an active role during the Iran-Iraq war. In those eight years it visited almost 40,000 Iranian and 67,000 Iraqi prisoners of war. It helped many of them return home. However, Iran reports that at least 11,000 Iranians are still missing. At least 375,000 Iraqis are too, but the number could be closer to a million.

The new agreement with the ICRC is helping families. Unfortunately, exact records of soldiers and civilians who are missing do not seem to exist. However, under the new agreement the ICRC is allowing Iran and Iraq to collect and share information. It also is leading to the exchange and identification of bodies.

About a million people died in the Iran-Iraq war. The families of those who died mourned their loss, but their tragedy lies in the past. It is different for the families of the missing though, because their pain is still present. Finally the ICRC's work is bringing them information and an end to their wondering and suffering.

Name _____ Date _____

REACTION GUIDE

Directions: <u>Now that you have read</u> "Families of Missing Persons Get Help," reread the statements below. Then think about how the author would feel about these statements. If you think the author would agree, put a check on the line before the number. Then, below the statement, copy the words, phrases, or sentences in the article that tell you the author's real views.

_____ **1.** Many people besides soldiers are lost in wars.

Article notes: _____

_____

_____

_____ **2.** Losing a relative is sad but not much of a practical problem.

Article notes: _____

_____

_____

_____ **3.** It is okay to kill civilians during a war if it helps end the conflict sooner.

Article notes: _____

_____

_____

WORDSTORM

Directions: It's good to know more than just the dictionary definition of a word. A wordstorm lets you write down information that helps you understand what a word means, how it's related to other words, and how to use it in different ways.

What is the word?

prisoner
_____

Copy the sentence from the text in which the word is used:

_____

_____

What are some other words or phrases that mean the same thing?

_____

What are three problems that the families of prisoners might have?

1. _____ 2. _____ 3. _____

Name three people who would likely use this word other than

teachers.

1. _____ 2. _____ 3. _____

Draw a picture that reminds you of the word "prisoner" below:

TIME MY READ # 1

Directions: With a partner, you will see how many words you can read correctly in 45 seconds. As you read, your partner will put an "X" through any word read incorrectly. Then your partner will read while you keep score. When you have both read, trade your books or papers. Count the total number of words you read correctly. Write this score at the bottom of your page.

WORD COUNT

relatives property flee agreement records remarrying exchange civilians	8
targets mortuaries scientists warfare prisoners separated victims villages	16
exact reunites inheritance practical mourned relatives thousands victims	24
relatives property flee agreement records remarrying exchange civilians	32
targets mortuaries scientists warfare prisoners separated victims villages	40
exact reunites inheritance practical mourned relatives thousands victims	48
relatives property flee agreement records remarrying exchange civilians	56
targets mortuaries scientists warfare prisoners separated victims villages	64
exact reunites inheritance practical mourned relatives thousands victims	72
relatives property flee agreement records remarrying exchange civilians	80

Number of words read correctly _____.

ECHO READING

Directions: When you read, you should make breaks between groups of words. As the teacher reads each phrase, repeat aloud what was read and underline that phrase. Then you will read the whole sentence aloud together. The first sentence has been underlined for you.

Since 1863 the International Committee of the Red Cross (ICRC) has helped victims of war all over the world. In fact, humanitarian law gives the ICRC the power to protect the dignity of the victims of war. That includes identifying missing persons.

The ICRC gathers all the information that it can about missing persons. It uses records from governments and from Red Cross workers who visit prisons, hospitals and mortuaries. When it identifies someone, it tries to reach the family. It sends information out through its own Web site, radio and printed messages. If it can, it contacts families directly. When things go well, it reunites families.

GET A CONTEXT CLUE

Directions: Below are sentences from "Families of Missing Persons Get Help." Read the sentence. Look back in the article and read the paragraph the sentence is in. Circle what you think is the best answer to each question.

"In 2008 Iraq and Iran signed an *agreement* to work with the Red Cross to find those missing persons."

1. The word "agreement" means:

   A. contract
   B. law
   C. petition
   D. lease

"Because of the many wars around the world, scientists have become more and more ex*act*."

2. The word "exact" means:

   A. precise or correct
   B. patient
   C. relaxed
   D. worried

"When things go well, it *reunites* families."

3. The word "reunites" means:

   A. reorganizes
   B. finds missing people
   C. brings family members together
   D. respects family members

"They also worry that the relative might be alive, but suffering *horribly* in a prison or hospital."

4. The word "horribly" means:

   A. unwillingly
   B. frequently
   C. terribly
   D. sadly

"It delays the *inheritance* of land, property and money."

5. The word "inheritance" means:

   A. sale
   B. farming
   C. fight for
   D. property passed at the owner's death

"The families of those who died *mourned* their loss, but their tragedy lies in the past."

6. The word "mourned" means:

   A. talked about
   B. fought over
   C. felt sad about; grieved
   D. celebrated

WORD CHOICE

Directions: As you read this piece, you will find blanks for missing words. Three words are listed after the blank. One of these is correct. <u>Read the rest of the sentence past the blank to figure out which is the correct word</u>. Write it in the blank.

The ICRC works with countries to get information about

_____ (misses, missed, missing) persons. They include

soldiers who _____ (might had, might have, might has) died

or _____ (became, become, becoming) prisoners. They also

include large numbers of civilians who _____ (have become,

have became, are becoming) targets in modern warfare. Civilians

_____ (die, death, dies) in attacks on their towns and

villages. Many _____ (fly, flea, flee) to other places for

safety, even to a neighboring country. Too often small children

_____ (become, became, becoming) separated from

_____ (there, their, they're) families.

The _____ (identify, identification, identity) of the dead

takes time. Because of the many wars around the world,

scientists _____ (have become, have became, have

becoming) more and more exact. They take DNA blood samples

from family members in order to help _____ (identify,

identifying, identifies) a body.

LOOK WHO'S TALKING

Directions: Number the paragraphs in the article. Below are sentences from "Families of Missing Persons Get Help." Number each paragraph. Look back in the article and re-read the paragraph in which you find the reference. Circle what you think is the best answer to each question.

1. In the first paragraph, the word "those" best refers to:

   A. the people in Iran
   B. people in Iraq
   C. the people in the Red Cross
   D. the civilians

2. In paragraph three, the word "they" refers to:

   A. the soldiers
   B. the civilians
   C. the missing people
   D. the Red Cross

3. In paragraph four, the word "they" refers to:

   A. the scientists
   B. the soldier
   C. the ICRC
   D. the civilians

4. In paragraph six, references to "they" are about:

   A. the ICRC
   B. the relatives
   C. the scientists
   D. the civilians

5. In paragraph seven the references to "it" are about:

   A. the relatives
   B. the missing people
   C. the civilians
   D. the scientists

6. In paragraph ten, the word "them" in the final sentence refers to:

   A. the relatives
   B. the scientists
   C. families
   D. the ICRC

Name _____ Date _____

NOTE MAKING

Directions: Read the key words on the left side of the chart below. Then add notes that answer the question in parentheses under the key word.

ICRC's purpose

(What?)

Helping victims of war

(How?)

Problems

(Which?)

Iran-Iraq War prisoners

(How many?)

New agreement

(What?)

"Families of Missing Persons Get Help"

IS THAT A FACT?

Directions: Read the definitions of a <u>fact</u> and an <u>inference</u> below. Then read the paragraph that follows. At the bottom of the page, write an "F" on the blank if a sentence is a fact or an "I" if it is an inference. Use the following definitions:

<u>Fact</u> – a statement that can be proven to be true from the article.

<u>Inference</u> – a guess as to what MIGHT be true.

"The new agreement with the ICRC will help families. Unfortunately, exact records of soldiers and civilians who are missing do not seem to exist. However, under the new agreement the ICRC will help Iran and Iraq collect and share information. It will also help with the exchange of information and bodies. About a million people died in the Iran-Iraq War. The families of those who died mourned their loss. But it is different for the families of the missing because their pain is still present. The ICRC's work will bring them information to end their suffering."

_____ **1.** The ICRC has become more efficient in locating missing people.

_____ **2.** The ICRC has a high level of international support.

_____ **3.** Civilians are often casualties of war.

_____ **4.** The Iraq-Iran War killed about a million people, including soldiers.

_____ **5.** The ICRC seeks to help people in difficult times.

_____ **6.** Countries that once fought each other will share information after their war.

TIME MY READ # 2

Directions: With a partner, you will see how many words you can read correctly in 45 seconds. As you read, your partner will put an "X" through any word read incorrectly. Then your partner will read while you keep score. When you have both read, trade your books or papers. Count the total number of words you read correctly. Write this score at the bottom of your page.

WORD COUNT

relatives property flee agreement records remarrying exchange civilians	8
targets mortuaries scientists warfare prisoners separated victims villages	16
exact reunites inheritance practical mourned relatives thousands victims	24
relatives property flee agreement records remarrying exchange civilians	32
targets mortuaries scientists warfare prisoners separated victims villages	40
exact reunites inheritance practical mourned relatives thousands victims	48
relatives property flee agreement records remarrying exchange civilians	56
targets mortuaries scientists warfare prisoners separated victims villages	64
exact reunites inheritance practical mourned relatives thousands victims	72
relatives property flee agreement records remarrying exchange civilians	80

Number of words read correctly _____. Is the score higher

than it was in Time My Read #1? _____

MAKE A SPACE

Directions: Below are sentences that are missing punctuation and capitalization. First, draw slash marks (/) between the words. Then rewrite each sentence in the space below it, filling in the missing punctuation and capitalization.

Example:

the/new/agreement/with/the/icrc/will/help/families

The new agreement with the ICRC will help families.

1. whencountriesareatwarmanysoldiersandciviliansgomissing

_____

_____

2. civilianshavebecometargetsinmodernwarfare

_____

_____

3. havingfamilymembersmissingaffectsthepracticalpartsofdailylife

_____

_____

4. since1863theinternationalcommitteeoftheredcrosshashelpedvictimsofwarallovertheworld

_____

_____

WORD PARTS

Directions: A suffix is added to the end of a base word to change how it's used in a sentence. Suffixes do this in many ways. For example, the suffix **–an** can turn a **noun** into an **adjective.** The noun "Mexico" becomes the adjective "Mexican," describing someone from Mexico. The suffix **–an** and the suffix **–ian** can also describe one who *is, practices, or works* with the base word. For example, an "electric**ian**" works with the base word "electricity." Write a definition of the words below. Look up the word or ask a partner if needed.

1. **Iranian** – _____

2. **authoritarian** – _____

3. **Costa Rican** – _____

4. **barbarian** – _____

5. **musician** – _____

6. **beautician** – _____

7. **Republican** – _____

8. **optician** – _____

9. **partisan** – _____

10. **humanitarian** – _____

Directions: Draw pictures to show the meanings of 2 of these words.

"Families of Missing Persons Get Help"

ICRC WORD PUZZLE

Directions: Complete the crossword puzzle.

Across

1. terribly or badly
2. correct or precise
7. property passed at the owner's death
8. a strong supporter of a political party
9. a person kept against his or her wishes

Down

1. person who wants to improve others' lives
3. a contract
4. a savage or uncivilized person
5. to bring people back together
6. felt sad about; grieved

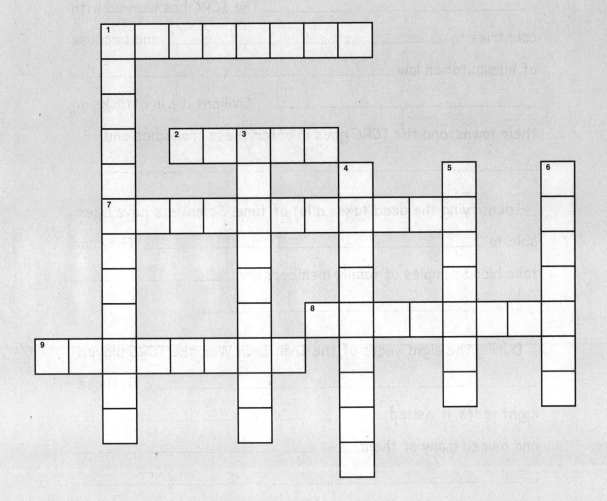

Word List

| MOURNED | AGREEMENT | BARBARIAN | HORRIBLY | PRISONER |
| HUMANITARIAN | REUNITE | INHERITANCE | EXACT | PARTISAN |

WRITING FRAME

Directions: Below is a writing frame. Use your knowledge and information from the article to complete the frame below.

When countries are at war, many soldiers and civilians go

missing. That happened to _____

during the Iran-Iraq War. Since 1863 the International

Committee of the Red Cross (ICRC) has _____

_____. The ICRC has worked with

countries to _____, and because

of humanitarian law _____

_____. Civilians die in attacks on

their towns, and the ICRC goes in after these tragedies and

_____.

Identifying the dead takes a lot of time. Scientists have been

able to _____. They can

take blood samples of family members and _____

_____.

During the eight years of the Iraq-Iran War, the ICRC played

_____. In those

eight years, it visited _____

and helped many of them _____

_____.

TAKE A STAND

Directions: People often have different feelings, or opinions, about the same thing. A "debate" is when people argue their different ideas. A good, persuasive argument has the following:

Facts – statements that can be proven to be true.

Statistics – research from a scientific study that uses numbers.

Examples – stories from the world that support an opinion.

You and a partner are going to debate two of your other classmates. The topic you are going to debate is the following:

It is okay to kill civilians during a war if it ends the conflict sooner.

Decide whether you agree or disagree with this statement. Then answer these questions in order to win your debate.

1. What are your 2 strongest points to persuade the other side?
(You can do Internet research to include facts, statistics, and examples.)

A. _____

B. _____

2. What will the other side say to argue against point A?

_____

_____

3. What will the other side say to argue against point B?

_____

_____

4. What will you say to prove the other side's arguments are wrong?

_____

_____

_____

ASSESSMENT

Comprehension: Answer the questions about the passage below.

The ICRC gathers all the information it can about missing persons. It uses records from governments and from Red Cross workers who visit hospitals and mortuaries. When it identifies someone, it tries to reach the family. Relatives suffer emotional pain when they don't know the fate of a loved one. They worry that the relative might be dead and lying in an unmarked grave. They also worry that a relative could be suffering horribly in a hospital or prison. The new agreement between Iraq and Iran will help the ICRC locate many more people.

1. How would you describe the work of the ICRC?

_____

_____

2. What is especially hard for relatives during warfare?

_____

_____

3. What was the author's purpose for writing about the ICRC?

_____

_____

Fluency: The words in the two sentences are all connected. The sentences are also missing punctuation and capitalization. Draw slash marks (/) between the words. Then rewrite the sentence, filling in the punctuation and capitalization.

1. manyfamiliesstilldonotknowwhathappenedtotheirrelatives

_____

_____

2. havingamissingrelativealsoaffectspracticalpartsofdailylife

_____

_____

ASSESSMENT

Fluency: Read the three sentences below. Imagine where you would pause within each sentence as you read it aloud. Draw a slash (/) mark between the phrases where you would pause. The first slash is done.

3. It delays / the inheritance of land, property, and money.

4. If it can, it contacts families directly, and reunites family members.

5. Relatives suffer emotional pain when they don't know the fate of a loved one.

Vocabulary: Based on what you have learned in this lesson, match the following words with their definitions. Write the letter of the definition on the blank in front of the word it defines.

1. _____ mourned   **A.** precise or correct

2. _____ agreement   **B.** a person kept against his or her wishes

3. _____ humanitarian   **C.** a strong supporter of a political party

4. _____ exact   **D.** to bring people back together

5. _____ partisan   **E.** felt sad about; grieved

6. _____ horribly   **F.** property passed at the owner's death

7. _____ barbarian   **G.** a contract

8. _____ inheritance   **H.** terribly or badly

9. _____ reunite   **I.** a savage or uncivilized person

10. _____ prisoner   **J.** a person who wants to improve others' lives

Name _____ Date _____

ANTICIPATION GUIDE

Directions: <u>Before</u> you read the article "Doping Damages Even the Best," read the statements below. If you agree with a statement, put a check on the line. Otherwise, leave it blank.

_____ **1.** Athletes have used drugs to help themselves for many years.

_____ **2.** Drugs to improve performance are not that harmful.

_____ **3.** Athletes who used steroids should lose any awards they won.

Once you have checked the statements above, tell why you agreed or disagreed with each statement in the section below.

1. _____

_____

2. _____

_____

3. _____

_____

In the box below, draw a picture of what you think this article is about.

What's Happening
IN THE USA?

By Lawrence Gable
© 2010 What's Happening Publications

Subject: Sports

Doping Damages Even the Best

Athletes always want to improve. Usually they do it through long hours of training. However, many of them have used drugs too. Now doping, the use of artificial stimulants, has become a problem for some of America's best athletes.

Doping includes serious health risks. Since some athletes are unwilling to take those risks, they cannot compete at the same level. International organizations for tennis, cycling, soccer and the Olympic Games have banned drugs, and America's pro sports leagues have too.

For many years athletes used things to ease pain or get energy. They used alcohol, caffeine and stimulants called amphetamines, which increase energy. In 1967 amphetamines caused the death of a cyclist during the Tour de France. Soon after that the Tour began testing riders for drugs.

Other forms of doping followed. In the 1970s athletes started taking steroids. Doctors use them to stimulate the growth of cells and bone. They make athletes larger and stronger, but they also present health risks. They cause mood swings and acne, as well as high blood pressure and heart damage.

Then in the 1980s a hormone called EPO became popular. It helps people with cancers and kidney diseases because it stimulates the production of red blood cells. In athletes it increases energy, but it thickens the blood and can lead to heart attacks.

Doping has made headlines in American sports. The track star Marion Jones always denied having used steroids. Then in 2007 she admitted that she had, in fact, used them. She also expressed her shame for having cheated in competitions and having lied to federal investigators. Ms. Jones ended up in prison for six months. The sport took away the titles that she had won since 2000, including five Olympic medals. The steroids that she took had come from a laboratory called Balco.

The investigation of Balco started with Ms. Jones's former coach. In 2003 he sent a sample of a steroid from Balco to the U.S. Anti-Doping Agency. Investigators then raided the lab and found that it had sent steroids to athletes.

The investigation also led some athletes to testify before a grand jury. One was Ms. Jones. Another was the baseball player Barry Bonds, who swore that he never had knowingly used steroids. However, the government said that investigators had found a positive test for steroids when they raided the Balco lab. The government accused him of having lied too, and plans to put him on trial.

A world-class American cyclist also has had problems. Floyd Landis won the 2006 Tour de France, but during the race he tested positive for doping. He denied having used steroids, but the race's officials took his title away. He served a two-year ban from racing until 2009. In 2010 he finally admitted to doping, and he accused other riders from his old team of doping too.

In 2007 a new American cycling team took a strong stand against doping. Team Slipstream's anti-doping program tested its riders 1,200 times in its first season. The team wanted to win races, but not at the cost of its riders' health. It also hoped to gain fans who believe in fair competition.

Doping is certainly a health issue. Athletes of all ages should not have to take harmful drugs in order to compete. It is also a character issue, since it is cheating. Doping charges have damaged the reputations of terrific athletes. In the end, athletes may decide that anything they achieve while doping feels shameful after all.

Name _____ Date _____

REACTION GUIDE

Directions: Now that you have read "Doping Damages Even the Best," reread the statements below. Then think about how the author would feel about these statements. If you think the author would agree, put a check on the line before the number. Then, below the statement, copy the words, phrases, or sentences in the article that tell you the author's real views.

_____ **1.** Athletes have used drugs to help themselves for many years.

Article notes: _____

_____

_____

_____ **2.** Drugs to improve performance are not that harmful.

Article notes: _____

_____

_____

_____ **3.** Athletes who used steroids should lose any awards they won.

Article notes: _____

_____

_____

PREDICTING ABC's

Directions: The article you are going to read is about athletes using drugs to improve their performance. See how many words you can fill in below about the use of steroids in sports. For example, put the word "muscle" in the M–O box. Try to put at least one word in every box.

A–C	D–F	G–I
J–L	**M–O**	**P–R**
S–T	**U–V**	**W–Z**

TIME MY READ # 1

Directions: With a partner, you will see how many words you can read correctly in 45 seconds. As you read, your partner will put an "X" through any word read incorrectly. Then your partner will read while you keep score. When you have both read, trade your books or papers. Count the total number of words you read correctly. Write this score at the bottom of your page.

WORD COUNT

stimulant serious health athletes amphetamines fatigue testing energy	8
cyclist investigators positive steroids stimulates accuses medals officials	16
admitted production thickens artificial increase supplied raided world-class	24
stimulant serious health athletes amphetamines fatigue testing energy	32
cyclist investigators positive steroids stimulates accuses medals officials	40
admitted production thickens artificial increase supplied raided world-class	48
stimulant serious health athletes amphetamines fatigue testing energy	56
cyclist investigators positive steroids stimulates accuses medals officials	64
admitted production thickens artificial increase supplied raided world-class	72
stimulant serious health athletes amphetamines fatigue testing energy	80

Number of words read correctly _____.

ECHO READING

Directions: Your teacher will read aloud the text below. Listen carefully. Draw lines under the words he or she groups together. The first sentence has been done for you.

Athletes constantly want to improve their performances.
Usually they do it through long hours of training and practice.
However, many of them have improved through drugs too. Now
doping, the use of artificial stimulants, has become a problem for
some of America's most famous athletes.

Doping includes serious health risks. Since some athletes are
unwilling to take those risks, they find themselves unable to
compete at the same level. International organizations that
govern tennis, cycling, soccer, and the Olympic Games have banned
it. America's pro sports leagues have banned it too.

For many years athletes used things to ease pain and get
energy. They used alcohol, caffeine, and stimulants called
amphetamines. But amphetamines caused death to some athletes.

GET A CONTEXT CLUE

Directions: Below are sentences from "Doping Damages Even the Best." Read the sentence. Look back in the article and read the paragraph the sentence is in. Circle what you think is the best answer to each question.

"Now doping, the use of artificial *stimulants,* has become a problem for some of America's best athletes."

1. The word "stimulant" means:

A. increase energy
B. make one sleepy
C. bring peace of mind
D. fight disease

"Since some athletes are unwilling to take those *risks,* they can't compete at the same level. "

2. The term "risks" means:

A. opportunities for fame
B. awards
C. challenges
D. chances of injury

"Other forms of *doping* followed."

3. The word "doping" means:

A. being stupid
B. lying
C. using drugs
D. cheating

"The investigation also led some athletes to *testify* before a grand jury."

4. The word "testify" means:

A. speak the truth
B. lie
C. take a test
D. sit

"A *world-class* American cyclist also has had problems."

5. The word "world-class" means:

A. good
B. foreign
C. student
D. one of the very best

"Doping is certainly a health *issue.*"

6. The word "issue" means:

A. disease
B. topic or subject
C. sport
D. choice

Name _____ Date _____

WORD MAP

Directions: Follow the directions to map the word in the box below.

stimulant

List 2 more words
that mean the same.

List 2 more things that
are stimulants.

List 2 opposites or
non-examples.

energy

coffee

decaf coffee

Draw a picture below to help
you remember the meaning.

Write a definition IN
YOUR OWN WORDS.

LOOK WHO'S TALKING

Directions: Below are sentences from "Doping Damages Even the Best." Number each paragraph. Look back in the article and re-read the paragraph in which you find the reference. Circle what you think is the best answer to each question.

1. In the second paragraph, the word "they" best refers to:

A. the international organizations
B. the athletes
C. pro sports leagues
D. the Olympics

2. In paragraph four, the word "them" refers to:

A. the drugs
B. the athletes
C. the cyclists
D. the stimulants

3. In paragraph five, the word "it" refers to:

A. the cells
B. the EPO hormone
C. the kidney disease
D. the cancer

4. In paragraph seven, the word "it" refers to:

A. the lab
B. the agency
C. the steroids
D. the U.S.

5. In paragraph eight the word "they" refers to:

A. the athletes
B. the Agency
C. the investigators
D. the lab

6. In paragraph ten, the repeated word "it" best refers to:

A. Slipstream
B. the team
C. riders' health
D. the steroids

HOW'S IT ORGANIZED?

This article is organized in **chronological order,** *or in the time order that*

things happened.

Directions: Answer these questions in the spaces at the bottom.

1. What started the stimulant controversy in 1967?

2. What stimulant did athletes begin doing in the 1970s?

3. What were the risks of these new drugs?

4. What stimulants became popular in the 1980s?

5. How did the Olympics react to Marion Jones's confession?

6. What did the U.S. Anti-Doping Agency learn in 2003?

7. Why did Floyd Landis lose his cyclist title in 2006?

8. Finally, who has taken a stand against doping since 2007?

Answers:

1.	
2.	
3.	
4.	
5.	
6.	
7.	
8.	

IS THAT A FACT?

Directions: Read the definitions of a <u>fact</u> and an <u>inference</u> below. Then read the paragraph that follows. At the bottom of the page, write an "F" on the blank if a sentence is a fact. Write an "I" if the sentence is an inference. Use the following definitions:

<u>Fact</u> – a statement that can be proven to be true from the article.

<u>Inference</u> – a guess as to what MIGHT be true.

> "Doping includes serious health risks. Since some athletes are unwilling to take those risks they cannot compete at the same level. International organizations for tennis, cycling, soccer, and the Olympic Games have banned drugs, and America's pro sports leagues have too. Doping is certainly a health issue. Athletes of all ages should not have to take harmful drugs in order to compete. It is also a character issue, since it is cheating. Doping charges have damaged the reputations of terrific athletes. In the end, athletes may decide that anything they achieve while doping feels shameful after all."

_____ **1.** Athletes are willing to risk their health in order to win.

_____ **2.** Athletes' reputations can be ruined if they are accused of using illegal drugs.

_____ **3.** Some athletes don't feel ashamed to use doping.

_____ **4.** The Olympics have made use of drugs illegal.

_____ **5.** Not all athletes are concerned about the effects of doping.

Name _____ Date _____

TIME MY READ # 2

Directions: With a partner, you will see how many words you can read correctly in 45 seconds. As you read, your partner will put an "X" through any word read incorrectly. Then your partner will read while you keep score. When you have both read, trade your books or papers. Count the total number of words you read correctly. Write this score at the bottom of your page.

WORD COUNT

stimulant serious health athletes amphetamines fatigue testing energy	8
cyclist investigators positive steroids stimulates accuses medals officials	16
admitted production thickens artificial increase supplied raided world-class	24
stimulant serious health athletes amphetamines fatigue testing energy	32
cyclist investigators positive steroids stimulates accuses medals officials	40
admitted production thickens artificial increase supplied raided world-class	48
stimulant serious health athletes amphetamines fatigue testing energy	56
cyclist investigators positive steroids stimulates accuses medals officials	64
admitted production thickens artificial increase supplied raided world-class	72
stimulant serious health athletes amphetamines fatigue testing energy	80

Number of words read correctly _____. Is the score higher

than it was in Time My Read #1?_____

MAKE A SPACE

Directions: Below are sentences that are missing punctuation and capitalization. First, draw slash marks (/) between the words. Then rewrite each sentence in the space below it, filling in the missing punctuation and capitalization.

Example:

now/doping/is/making/headlines/in/american/sports

Now doping is making headlines in American sports.

1. dopingortheuseofartificialstimulantshasbecomeaproblemforathletes

_____

_____

2. theamericancyclingteamhastakenastandagainsttheuseofdoping

_____

_____

3. athletesofallagesshouldnothavetousedopingtocompete

_____

_____

4. inathletesitincreasesenergybutthickensthebloodandleadstoheartattacks

_____

_____

WORD PARTS

Directions: A **base word** is a word that can stand alone. A **prefix** is a word part added to the beginning of a base word. For example, in the word **antitheft, theft** is the base word and **anti–** is the prefix added at the beginning. The prefix **anti–** means "against" or "opposite of." *Antitheft* means something that stops people from stealing. Write a definition for the words below on the line. Try <u>not</u> to use the base word in the definition. If you don't know the base word, such as *reform* in "antireform," look it up in a dictionary or ask a partner.

1. **antiaircraft** – _____

2. **antifogging** – _____

3. **antisocial** – _____

4. **antilock** – _____

5. **antimissile** – _____

6. **antiforeigner** – _____

7. **antifreeze** – _____

8. **antireform** – _____

9. **antiwar** – _____

10. **antimilitary** – _____

11. **antifungal** – _____

12. **antiperspirant** – _____

13. **antiterrorist** – _____

14. **antiglare** – _____

15. **antiregulatory** – _____

SUMMARIZING ABC's

Directions: Now that you've read the article about athletes using steroids, see how many words you can fill in the boxes below.

A–C	D–F	G–I
J–L	**M–O**	**P–R**
S–T	**U–V**	**W–Z**

SENTENCE SUMMARIES

Directions: Below are 4 key words from the article "Doping Damages Even the Best." Your job is to summarize, or restate, what you've learned in this article by using these 4 words or phrases in two sentences. Then, as a challenge, try to use all 4 words or phrases in one sentence to restate the article.

FOUR KEY WORDS OR PHRASES

stimulants   athletes
risks   investigations

Sentence Summaries:

1. _____

_____

2. _____

_____

Challenge Summary (All 4 words or phrases in one sentence!)

1. _____

_____

_____

TAKE A STAND

Directions: People often have different feelings, or opinions, about the same thing. A "debate" is when people argue their different ideas. A good, persuasive argument has the following:

Facts – statements that can be proven to be true.

Statistics – research from a scientific study that uses numbers.

Examples – stories from the world that support an opinion.

You and a partner are going to debate two of your other classmates. The topic you are going to debate is the following:

> *Athletes who used steroids should lose any awards they won.*

Decide whether you agree or disagree with this statement. Then answer these questions in order to win your debate.

1. What are your 2 strongest points to persuade the other side?
(You can do Internet research to include facts, statistics, and examples.)

A. _____

B. _____

2. What will the other side say to argue against point A?

_____

_____

3. What will the other side say to argue against point B?

_____

_____

4. What will you say to prove the other side's arguments are wrong?

_____

_____

Name _____ Date _____

ASSESSMENT

Comprehension: Answer the questions about the passage below.

"Doping is certainly a health issue. Athletes of all ages should not have to take harmful drugs in order to compete. It is also a character issue, since it is cheating. Doping charges have damaged the reputations of terrific athletes. In the end, athletes may decide that anything they achieve while doping feels shameful after all."

1. Why has doping become so tempting for athletes?

_____

_____

2. Why would people be concerned about an athlete's use of drugs?

_____

_____

3. Why do you think the author wrote this article about the subject?

_____

_____

Fluency: The words in the two sentences are all connected. The sentences are also missing punctuation and capitalization. Draw slash marks (/) between the words. Then rewrite the sentence, filling in the punctuation and capitalization.

1. inathletesitincreasesenergybutitthickensthebloodandcanleadtoheartattacks

_____

_____

2. floydlandisdeniedusingsteroidsandhasbeenbannedfromracing

_____

_____

ASSESSMENT

Fluency: Read the three sentences below. Imagine where you would pause within each sentence as you read it aloud. Draw a slash (/) mark between the phrases where you would pause. The first slash is done.

3. Since some athletes / are unwilling to take those risks, they can't compete at the same level.

4. Now the government says they found a positive test for steroids.

5. The team wants to win races, but not at the cost of the riders' health.

Vocabulary: Based on what you have learned in this lesson, match the following words with their definitions. Write the letter of the definition on the blank in front of the word it defines.

1. _____ stimulant   **A.** describing a gun that shoots down planes

2. _____ antisocial   **B.** using drugs or steroids

3. _____ doping   **C.** one of the best in the world

4. _____ antiforeigner   **D.** against someone from another country

5. _____ testify   **E.** something that may cause an injury

6. _____ antiperspirant   **F.** describing someone who likes to be alone

7. _____ issue   **G.** to speak the truth in court

8. _____ world-class   **H.** something that keeps one from sweating

9. _____ antiaircraft   **I.** something that increases energy

10. _____ risk   **J.** topic or subject

Name _____ Date _____

ANTICIPATION GUIDE

Directions: <u>Before</u> you read the article "The Outlook is Improving for Right Whales," read the statements below. If you agree with a statement, put a check on the line. Otherwise, leave it blank.

_____ **1.** Right whales are nearly extinct.

_____ **2.** Human hunters kill most right whales.

_____ **3.** If people need food, they should be allowed to eat endangered plants and animals.

Once you have checked the statements above, tell why you agreed or disagreed with each statement in the section below.

1. _____

_____

2. _____

_____

3. _____

_____

In the box below, draw a picture of what you think this article is about.

What's Happening
IN THE WORLD?

By Lawrence Gable
© *2010 What's Happening Publications*

Subject: Environment

The North Atlantic right whale is an endangered species. Researchers estimate their population at only around 325. However, in 2009 they got good news when they saw a record number of calves. They counted 39, and that was the best sign in centuries for the right whale's survival.

The right whale is easy to identify. It has a black body, and may have white patches on its underside. It can grow to 55 feet long and 70 tons. It does not have a dorsal fin on its back, but it has two blowholes that form a V-shaped blow of water and air. Growths on its head make one right whale look different from another.

Right whales prefer shallow waters. They swim slowly along the coastline and in large bays. They have no teeth. Instead they have large jaws made of whalebone. Hundreds of whalebone plates hang from their upper jaw. As the whale opens its mouth to feed, the plates filter food from the water.

The right whale's name came from whalers. The whales were easy targets because they are slow, swim close to shore and float when they are dead. In addition, their bodies contain large amounts of oil, meat and whalebone. Whalers thought they were "right" for hunting.

Whalers from America almost hunted the right whale to extinction. By 1750 the North Atlantic right whale's numbers were so low that whalers moved to the South Atlantic and South Pacific. By the early 20th century whalers had killed about 40,000 right whales in each ocean. They also had taken 15,000 in the North Atlantic.

The world decided to protect the right whale.

The Outlook is Improving for Right Whales

A worldwide ban on commercial hunting took effect in 1935. That stopped the population from getting smaller. Now Canadian and U.S. laws protect right whales. The U.S. put the right whale on the Endangered Species list in the 1970s.

The North Atlantic right whale still faces serious threats. They have only two predators, killer whales and humans. Researchers believe that killer whales do little damage. Even though humans no longer hunt the right whale, still their activities have killed too many.

Collisions with ships are the largest cause of right whale deaths along the Atlantic coast. Ships going in and out of harbors kill at least two or three a year. In 2008 new regulations went into effect. Now ships over 65 feet long must slow down. They also must sail in new shipping lanes that avoid areas where whales are.

The other great danger to right whales is entanglement in commercial fishing lines. Some whales drown because they get wrapped in thick ropes and nets. Others suffer from decreased mobility and infection. The number of entanglements has risen sharply in recent years.

Research and environmental organizations cooperate to help right whales. They use boats and planes to locate them, then report their locations so that ships can avoid them. They also have teams that free whales from fishing lines. Whenever possible, they take photos and enter them into a computer system.

According to the New England Aquarium, not a single North Atlantic right whale died because of humans in 2008. That was probably the first time since the 1600s. Although there are still dangers for them and their survival, the increased number of calves provides hope.

Name _____ Date _____

REACTION GUIDE

Directions: <u>Now that you have read</u> "The Outlook is Improving for Right Whales," reread the statements below. Then think about how the author would feel about these statements. If you think the author would agree, put a check on the line before the number. Then, below the statement, copy the words, phrases, or sentences in the article that tell you the author's real views.

_____ **1.** Right whales are nearly extinct.

Article notes: _____

_____

_____

_____ **2.** Human hunters kill most right whales.

Article notes: _____

_____

_____

_____ **3.** If people need food, they should be allowed to eat endangered plants and animals.

Article notes: _____

_____

_____

WORDSTORM

Directions: It's good to know more than just the dictionary definition of a word. A wordstorm lets you write down information that helps you understand what a word means, how it's related to other words, and how to use it in different ways.

What is the word?

endangered
_____

Copy the sentence from the text in which the word is used:

_____

_____

What are some other words or phrases that mean the same thing?

_____

What are three reasons why living things might be endangered?

1. _____ 2. _____ 3. _____

Name three people who would likely use this word other than

teachers.

1. _____ 2. _____ 3. _____

Draw a picture that reminds you of the word "endangered" below:

TIME MY READ # 1

Directions: With a partner, you will see how many words you can read correctly in 45 seconds. As you read, your partner will put an "X" through any word read incorrectly. Then your partner will read while you keep score. When you have both read, trade your books or papers. Count the total number of words you read correctly. Write this score at the bottom of your page.

WORD COUNT

population underside dorsal calves filter serious whaler regulations	8
survival collisions shipping plates distinctive estimate researchers oil	16
extinction species damage endangered aquarium commercial vessels mobility	24
population underside dorsal calves filter serious whaler regulations	32
survival collisions shipping plates distinctive estimate researchers oil	40
extinction species damage endangered aquarium commercial vessels mobility	48
population underside dorsal calves filter serious whaler regulations	56
survival collisions shipping plates distinctive estimate researchers oil	64
extinction species damage endangered aquarium commercial vessels mobility	72
population underside dorsal calves filter serious whaler regulations	80

Number of words read correctly _____.

ECHO READING

Directions: When you read, you should make breaks between groups of words. As the teacher reads each phrase, repeat aloud what was read and underline that phrase. Then you will read the whole sentence aloud together. The first sentence has been underlined for you.

The right whale's name came from whalers. The whales were easy targets because they are slow, swim close to shore, and float when they are dead. In addition, their bodies contain large amounts of oil, meat and whalebone. Whalers thought they were "right" for hunting.

Whalers from America almost hunted the right whale to extinction. By 1750 the North Atlantic right whale's numbers were so low that whalers moved to the South Atlantic and South Pacific. By the early 20th century whalers had killed about 40,000 right whales in each ocean. They had also taken 15,000 in the North Atlantic.

Name _____ Date _____

GET A CONTEXT CLUE

Directions: Below are sentences from "The Outlook is Improving for Right Whales."
Read the sentence. Look back in the article and read the paragraph the sentence is in.
Circle the best answer to each question.

"Researchers *estimate* their population at only around 325."

1. The word "estimate" means:

   A.   wish
   B.   firmly believe
   C.   guess based on information
   D.   hate

"Right whales prefer *shallow* waters."

2. The word "shallow" means:

   A.   deep
   B.   cold
   C.   fast
   D.   not deep

"A worldwide ban on commercial hunting *took effect* in 1935."

3. The phrase "took effect" means:

   A.   began
   B.   fell apart
   C.   ended
   D.   restarted

"The other great danger to right whales is *entanglement* in commercial fishing lines."

4. The word "entanglement" means:

   A.   being wrapped or trapped
   B.   swimming
   C.   sleeping
   D.   being found

"In 2008 new *regulations* went into effect."

5. The word "regulations" means:

   A.   statements
   B.   laws or rules
   C.   ideas
   D.   projects

"Research and environmental organizations *cooperate* to help right whales."

6. The word "cooperate" means:

   A.   argue about
   B.   try
   C.   work together
   D.   do research

WORD CHOICE

Directions: As you read this piece, you will find blanks for missing words. Three words are listed after the blank. One of these is correct. <u>Read the rest of the sentence past the blank to figure out which is the correct word</u>. Write it in the blank.

The world _____ (decides, deciding, decided) to protect

the right whale. A worldwide ban on commercial hunting

_____ (took, takes, taking) effect in 1935. That

_____ (stopped, stops, stopping) the population from

_____ (gets, got, getting) smaller. Now Canadian and U.S.

laws _____ (protect, protects, protecting) right whales. The

U.S. put the right whale on the _____ (endangering,

endangers, endangered) list in the 1970's. The whales

_____ (have, has, having) only two predators, killer whales

and humans. Researchers _____ (belief, believe, believing)

that killer whales do little damage. Even though humans no

longer _____ (hunting, hunters, hunt) the right whale, still

_____ (there, their, they're) activities have _____

(killed, kills, kill) too many.

LOOK WHO'S TALKING

Directions: Below are sentences from "The Outlook is Improving for Right Whales." Number each paragraph. Look back in the article and re-read the paragraph in which you find the reference. Circle what you think is the best answer to each question.

1. In the first paragraph, the word "they" best refers to:

A.   the whales
B.   the researchers
C.   the calves
D.   none of the above

2. In paragraph four, the second use of the word "they" refers to:

A.   the whales
B.   the whalers
C.   The bodies
D.   the heads

3. In paragraph seven, the word "they" refers to:

A.   the whalers
B.   the whales
C.   the humans
D.   the researchers

4. In paragraph eight, the word "they" refers to:

A.   the ships
B.   the researchers
C.   the whales
D.   none of the above

5. In paragraph ten the word "they" refers to:

A.   the whales
B.   the ships
C.   the organizations
D.   the locations

6. In paragraph eleven the word "them" refers to:

A.   the whales
B.   the organization
C.   the researchers
D.   the whalers

NOTE MAKING

Directions: Read the key **bold** words on the left side of the chart below. Then add notes that answer the question in parentheses under the key word.

Right whales

(What?)

Their name

(How?)

Hunted

(Where and why?)

Endangered

(By what?)

Saved from extinction

(How?)

"The Outlook is Improving for Right Whales"

IS THAT A FACT?

Directions: Read the definitions of a <u>fact</u> and an <u>inference</u> below. Then read the paragraph that follows. At the bottom of the page, write an "F "on the blank if a sentence is a fact or an "I" if it is an inference. Use the following definitions:

<u>Fact</u> – a statement that can be proven to be true from the article.

<u>Inference</u> – a guess as to what MIGHT be true.

"Research and environmental organizations cooperate to help right whales. They use boats and planes to locate them, and then report that information so that ships can avoid them. They also have teams that free whales from fishing lines. Whenever possible, they take photos and enter them in their computer system. According to the New England Aquarium, not a single right whale died because of humans in 2008. That was probably the first time since the 1600s."

_____ **1.** People are getting more concerned about the right whale.

_____ **2.** Agencies are using high-level technology to help the whales.

_____ **3.** The number of right whale deaths at the hands of humans is declining.

_____ **4.** Whales can die when they encounter fishing lines.

_____ **5.** No whales died at the hands of human beings in 2008.

_____ **6.** If ships get reports in time, they can avoid hitting whales.

MAKE A SPACE

Directions: Below are sentences that are missing punctuation and capitalization. First, draw slash marks (/) between the words. Then rewrite each sentence in the space below it, filling in the missing punctuation and capitalization.

Example:

now/the/whales/are/swimming/north/to/Canada

Now the whales are swimming north to Canada.

1. thenumberofentanglementshasrisensharplyinthelastdecade

_____

_____

2. researchandenvironmentalorganizationscooperatetohelprightwhales

_____

_____

3. nowshipsmustsailinlanestoavoidareaswherethewhalesare

_____

_____

4. aworldwidebanonhuntingtookplacein1935

_____

_____

Name _____ Date _____

TIME MY READ # 2

Directions: With a partner, you will see how many words you can read correctly in 45 seconds. As you read, your partner will put an "X" through any word read incorrectly. Then your partner will read while you keep score. When you have both read, trade your books or papers. Count the total number of words you read correctly. Write this score at the bottom of your page.

population underside dorsal calves filter serious whaler regulations	8
survival collisions shipping plates distinctive estimate researchers oil	16
extinction species damage endangered aquarium commercial vessels mobility	24
population underside dorsal calves filter serious whaler regulations	32
survival collisions shipping plates distinctive estimate researchers oil	40
extinction species damage endangered aquarium commercial vessels mobility	48
population underside dorsal calves filter serious whaler regulations	56
survival collisions shipping plates distinctive estimate researchers oil	64
extinction species damage endangered aquarium commercial vessels mobility	72
population underside dorsal calves filter serious whaler regulations	80

Number of words read correctly _____. Is the score higher

than it was in Time My Read #1?_____

WORD PARTS

Directions: A **base word** is a word that can stand alone. A **suffix** is a word part added to the end of a base word to change how the word is used in the sentence. The suffixes **-tion, -ation, -sion,** and **-cion** all change **verbs** to abstract **nouns.** The new noun can *express action* (revolution); or *tell what state something is in* (starvation). Write a definition of the words below. Try _not_ to use the base word in the definition. If you don't know the base word, such as revolt in "revolution," look it up in a dictionary or ask a partner.

1. extinction – _____

2. suspicion – _____

3. population – _____

4. confusion – _____

5. imagination – _____

6. organization – _____

7. decision – _____

8. instruction – _____

9. coercion – _____

10. regulation – _____

11. possession – _____

12. exploration – _____

13. aggression – _____

14. temptation – _____

15. exclusion – _____

WHALES CROSSWORD PUZZLE

Directions: Complete the crossword puzzle.

Across

1 to lay open or expose to harm
4 the total number of something, such as people or animals
7 to guess based on information
8 not deep
9 the state of being completely killed off
10 began (2 words)

Down

2 a trap
3 to work together
5 a group of people united for a purpose
6 a law or ruler

Word List

ESTIMATE	ENDANGER	ENTANGLEMENT	ORGANIZATION	POPULATION
EXTINCTION	SHALLOW	REGULATION	COOPERATE	TOOKEFFECT

WRITING FRAME

Directions: Below is a writing frame. Use your knowledge and information from the article to complete the frame below.

> The North Atlantic right whale is an endangered species.
> Researchers estimate that _____
> However, _____ have appeared and that is good
> news. The right whale is easy to spot because _____
> _____, and _____
> _____. The right whale was given that
> name because _____. Whalers from
> America almost _____. But now,
> the world has decided to _____.
> There now is a _____ on commercial hunting that
> took effect in _____. That resulted in the
> population's getting _____. Now
> Canadian and U.S. laws protect the whales by putting them
> _____. Environmental and
> research organizations _____.
> They use boats and planes to locate the whales so that ships
> avoid them.

"The Outlook is Improving for Right Whales"

Name _____ Date _____

TAKE A STAND

Directions: People often have different feelings, or opinions, about the same thing. A "debate" is when people argue their different ideas. A good, persuasive argument has the following:

Facts – statements that can be proven to be true.

Statistics – research from a scientific study that uses numbers.

Examples – stories from the world that support an opinion.

You and a partner are going to debate two of your other classmates. The topic you are going to debate is the following:

If very hungry, people should eat endangered plants and animals.

Decide whether you agree or disagree with this statement. Then answer these questions in order to win your debate.

1. What are your 2 strongest points to persuade the other side?
(You can do Internet research to include facts, statistics, and examples.)

A. _____

B. _____

2. What will the other side say to argue against point A?

_____

_____

3. What will the other side say to argue against point B?

_____

_____

4. What will you say to prove the other side's arguments are wrong?

_____

_____

ASSESSMENT

Comprehension: Answer the questions about the passage below.

Whalers from America almost hunted the right whale to extinction. By 1750 the North Atlantic right whale's numbers were so low that whalers moved to the South Atlantic and the South Pacific. By the early 20th century whalers had killed about 40,000 right whales in each ocean. They also had taken 15,000 in the North Atlantic. Entanglements in nets from commercial fishing ships are now one of the largest causes of whales' death. They get wrapped in thick nets and drown, or they suffer from infections. The number of entanglements has risen recently.

1. What caused right whales to become nearly extinct in the past?

_____

_____

2. What dangers do right whales face today?

_____

_____

3. What was the author's purpose for writing about right whales?

_____

_____

Fluency: The words in the two sentences are all connected. The sentences are also missing punctuation and capitalization. Draw slash marks (/) between the words. Then rewrite the sentence, filling in the punctuation and capitalization.

1. shipsgoinginandoutofharborskilltwoorthreewhaleseachyear

_____

_____

2. indecembernewregulationswentintoeffectandnowshipsmustsailinareasthatavoidthewhales

_____

_____

Name _____ Date _____

Fluency: Read the three sentences below. Imagine where you would pause within each sentence as you read it aloud. Draw a slash (/) mark between the phrases where you would pause. The first slash is done.

3. Hundreds of whalebone plates / hang from their upper jaw.

4. Now ships over sixty-five feet must slow down.

5. The North Atlantic right whale still faces serious threats.

Vocabulary: Based on what you have learned in this lesson, match the following words with their definitions. Write the letter of the definition on the blank in front of the word it defines.

1. _____ endanger   **A.** to work together

2. _____ regulation   **B.** being trapped or wrapped

3. _____ estimate   **C.** not deep

4. _____ organization   **D.** to guess based on information

5. _____ cooperate   **E.** expose to harm

6. _____ took effect   **F.** a group of people united for a purpose

7. _____ population   **G.** a law or rule

8. _____ entanglement   **H.** the total number of something

9. _____ shallow   **I.** began

10. _____ extinction   **J.** the state of being completely killed off

Name _____ Date _____

ANTICIPATION GUIDE

Directions: <u>Before</u> you read the article "Court Gives Saggy Pants a Lift," read the statements below. If you agree with a statement, put a check on the line. Otherwise, leave it blank.

_____ **1.** Certain groups have the right to tell people what to wear.

_____ **2.** Laws banning fashion are against our freedom of expression.

_____ **3.** A city should have the right to ban fashion that is offensive.

Once you have checked the statements above, tell why you agreed or disagreed with each statement in the section below.

1. _____

_____

2. _____

_____

3. _____

_____

In the box below, draw a picture of what you think this article is about.

_____

"Court Gives Saggy Pants a Lift"

What's Happening
IN THE USA?

By Lawrence Gable
© 2010 What's Happening Publications

Subject: Human Rights

Court Gives Saggy Pants a Lift

In recent years boys and young men have been wearing their pants low. Often their boxer shorts show. This may be a cool fashion to them, but many towns think it is indecent. Riviera Beach, Florida, made it illegal, but the county's public defender challenged that law a year later.

There are decency laws everywhere in the U.S. They protect people from things that are morally offensive. The laws apply to things like public behavior, art, TV, and even personalized license plates.

Many places also have dress codes. Some professions require workers to wear uniforms, and some employers limit what employees can wear. Pro basketball players follow a dress code off the court. Schools can restrict what students and teachers wear. In general, dress codes apply to private settings.

The attempts by cities to ban saggy pants fall somewhere between dress codes and decency laws. Cities are not trying to create public dress codes. They already have decency laws, but they do not cover boxer shorts. Some people find the fashion disgusting and want to ban it.

A number of places have banned saggy pants. Their laws define how low pants can be. Officials in Augusta, Georgia, considered changing its decency law. It would have made "exposure of the buttocks" illegal, but not exposing boxer shorts. City officials voted not to change the law after all.

The American Civil Liberties Union (ACLU) opposes laws against saggy pants. The organization has offered to represent individuals in court. It believes that such laws go against the right to freedom of expression. The ACLU also fears that cities could use them unfairly against young Black men and the poor.

There is a certain racial origin to the style. Hip-hop artists made sagging pants popular. They may have taken the style from prisons where prisoners do not have belts. For quite a while the style was popular mostly with young Blacks, but now many others also wear saggy pants.

In 2008 people in Riviera Beach voted for a law against sagging pants. In the first year the city charged nearly two dozen young men. After a 17-year-old had to spend a night in jail, a judge declared the ban unconstitutional. However, the city kept its law, so the public defender's office went to court.

The public defenders wanted the court to drop the charges against some young men. They argued that the U.S. Constitution protects fashion as freedom of expression. One witness, a fashion instructor, told the court that saggy pants have spread into the mainstream. She showed photos of David Beckham and Zac Efron wearing pants low.

Plenty of people argue that laws should stay away from fashion. People have different tastes in what looks good. Some other clothes show a lot of bare skin or undergarments, but they are not indecent. People who do not like sagging pants, but do not want laws against them, know that they will go away because fashions change.

In April 2008 a judge ruled against Riviera Beach's law. She said that the style may be "tacky or distasteful," but that the Fourteenth Amendment protects such choices. Courts may rule differently in other places in the future. In Riviera Beach, though, the court threw out the law against saggy pants.

Name _____ Date _____

Directions: Now that you have read "Court Gives Saggy Pants a Lift," reread the statements below. Then think about how the author would feel about these statements. If you think the author would agree, put a check on the line before the number. Then, below the statement, copy the words, phrases, or sentences in the article that tell you the author's real views.

_____ **1.** Certain groups have the right to tell people what to wear.

Article notes: _____

_____

_____

_____ **2.** Laws banning fashion are against our freedom of expression.

Article notes: _____

_____

_____

_____ **3.** A city should have the right to ban fashion that is offensive.

Article notes: _____

_____

_____

PREDICTING ABC's

Directions: The article you are going to read is about "dress codes." See how many words you can fill in below about banning clothes in certain situations, such as at school. For example, put the word "flip flops" in the D–F box. Try to put at least one word in every box.

A–C	D–F	G–I
J–L	**M–O**	**P–R**
S–T	**U–V**	**W–Z**

Name _____ Date _____

TIME MY READ # 1

Directions: With a partner, you will see how many words you can read correctly in 45 seconds. As you read, your partner will put an "X" through any word read incorrectly. Then your partner will read while you keep score. When you have both read, trade your books or papers. Count the total number of words you read correctly. Write this score at the bottom of your page.

WORD COUNT

decency fashion opposes ban undergarments fashion defenders exposure	8
indecent exposing charged buttocks disgusting represents freedom expression	16
style defenders disgusting bare charges amendment choices uniforms	24
decency fashion opposes ban undergarments fashion defenders exposure	32
indecent exposing charged buttocks disgusting represents freedom expression	40
style defenders disgusting bare charges amendment choices uniforms	48
decency fashion opposes ban undergarments fashion defenders exposure	56
indecent exposing charged buttocks disgusting represents freedom expression	64
style defenders disgusting bare charges amendment choices uniforms	72
decency fashion opposes ban undergarments fashion defenders exposure	80

Number of words read correctly _____.

"Court Gives Saggy Pants a Lift"

ECHO READING

Directions: When you read, you should make breaks between groups of words. As the teacher reads each phrase, repeat aloud what was read and underline that phrase. Then you will read the whole sentence aloud together. The first sentence has been underlined for you.

<u>Many places also have dress codes.</u> Some professions require workers to wear uniforms, and some employers limit what employees can wear. Pro basketball players follow a dress code off the court. Schools can restrict what students and teachers wear. In general, dress codes apply to private settings.

A number of places have banned saggy pants. Their laws define how low pants can be. In 2008 officials in Augusta, Georgia considered changing its decency law. It would have made "exposure of the buttocks" illegal, but not exposing boxer shorts. City officials voted not to change the law after all.

Plenty of people argue that laws should stay away from fashion. People have different tastes in what looks good. Some clothes show a lot of bare skin or undergarments, but they are not indecent.

GET A CONTEXT CLUE

Directions: Below are sentences from "Courts Give Saggy Pants a Lift." Read the sentence. Look back in the article and read the paragraph the sentence is in. Then circle what you think is the best answer to each question.

"They protect people from things that are morally *offensive*."

1. The word "offensive" means:

   A. acceptable
   B. extreme
   C. insulting
   D. rarely done

"Schools can *restrict* what students and teachers wear."

2. The word "restrict" means:

   A. shock
   B. warn
   C. control or limit
   D. question

"The attempts by cities to ban saggy pants fall between dress codes and *decency* laws."

3. The term "decency" means:

   A. what is helpful
   B. what is unusual
   C. what is proper for most
   D. what is likeable

"A number of places have *banned* baggy pants."

4. The word "banned" means:

   A. no longer possible
   B. sometimes allowed
   C. approved
   D. no longer allowed

"After a 17 year old spent the night in jail, a judge declared the ban *unconstitutional*."

5. The word "unconstitutional" means:

   A. ordinary
   B. promoting a law or code
   C. turning things around
   D. violating people's rights

"One witness, a fashion instructor, told the court that saggy pants have spread into the *mainstream*."

6. The word "mainstream" means:

   A. the general population
   B. the younger generation
   C. only people in Maine
   D. hip hop artists

WORD MAP

Directions: Follow the directions to map the word in the box below.

> **freedom**

List 2 more words that mean the same.

List 2 more examples of freedoms.

List 2 opposites or non-examples.

> right

> Freedom of speech

> restriction

Draw a picture below to help you remember the meaning.

Write a definition IN YOUR OWN WORDS.

LOOK WHO'S TALKING

Directions: Below are sentences from "Courts Give Saggy Pants a Lift." Number each paragraph. Look back in the article and re-read the paragraph in which you find the sentence. Circle what you think is the best answer to each question.

1. **In the first paragraph, the word "their" best refers to:**

   A. the county
   B. public defenders
   C. young men
   D. law

2. **In paragraph four, the word "they" refers to:**

   A. the cities
   B. the laws
   C. the dress codes
   D. the people

3. **In paragraph five, the word "it" refers to:**

   A. the laws
   B. the people
   C. the exposure
   D. the city officials

4. **In paragraph seven the word "others" refers to:**

   A. the hip-hop artists
   B. regular people
   C. prisoners
   D. young African-Americans

5. **In paragraph nine the word "they" refers to:**

   A. the witnesses
   B. the court
   C. the David Beckham and Zac Efron
   D. the public defenders

6. **In paragraph ten the word "they" refers to:**

   A. the fashion
   B. the saggy pants
   C. the people who don't like saggy pants
   D. the laws

HOW'S IT ORGANIZED?

This article is organized as **cause and effect**, or *one thing happens, which causes an effect, or reaction.* This reaction often starts another event.

Directions: Answer these questions in the spaces at the bottom.

1. What is the cause of the controversy in this article?

2. What effect does this fashion have on some people?

3. How did Augusta, Georgia, respond to the controversy?

4. How did the ACLU react to Augusta's action?

5. How did Riviera Beach, CA, respond to the controversy?

6. What event brought the controversy to court in Riviera Beach?

7. What did the judge decide about Riviera Beach's law?

Answers:

1.	
2.	
3.	
4.	
5.	
6.	
7.	

IS THAT A FACT?

Directions: Read the definitions of a <u>fact</u> and an <u>inference</u> below. Then read the paragraph that follows. At the bottom of the page, write an "F" on the blank if a sentence is a fact. Write an "I" if the sentence is an inference. Use the following definitions:

<u>Fact</u> – a statement that can be proven to be true from the article.

<u>Inference</u> – a guess as to what MIGHT be true.

"The attempts by cities to ban saggy pants fall somewhere between dress codes and decency laws. Cities are not trying to create public dress codes. They already have public decency laws, but they do not cover boxer shorts. Some people find the fashion disgusting and want to ban it.

A number of places have banned saggy pants. Their laws define how low pants can be. The American Civil Liberties Union (ACLU) opposes laws against saggy pants."

_____ **1.** Some people feel they have a right to tell people how to dress.

_____ **2.** Some people are disgusted by this fashion.

_____ **3.** The ACLU does not want bans on saggy pants.

_____ **4.** Cities do not have the same laws about saggy pants.

_____ **5.** The people who offend the public are usually males.

TIME MY READ # 2

Directions: With a partner, you will see how many words you can read correctly in 45 seconds. As you read, your partner will put an "X" through any word read incorrectly. Then your partner will read while you keep score. When you have both read, trade your books or papers. Count the total number of words you read correctly. Write this score at the bottom of your page.

WORD COUNT

decency fashion opposes ban undergarments fashion defenders exposure	8
indecent exposing charged buttocks disgusting represents freedom expression	16
style defenders disgusting bare charges amendment choices uniforms	24
decency fashion opposes ban undergarments fashion defenders exposure	32
indecent exposing charged buttocks disgusting represents freedom expression	40
style defenders disgusting bare charges amendment choices uniforms	48
decency fashion opposes ban undergarments fashion defenders exposure	56
indecent exposing charged buttocks disgusting represents freedom expression	64
style defenders disgusting bare charges amendment choices uniforms	72
decency fashion opposes ban undergarments fashion defenders exposure	80

Number of words read correctly _____. Is the score higher

than it was in Time My Read #1?_____

MAKE A SPACE

Directions: Below are sentences that are missing punctuation and capitalization. First, draw slash marks (/) between the words. Then rewrite each sentence in the space below it, filling in the missing punctuation and capitalization.

Example:

there/are/decency/laws/everywhere/in/the/U.S.

There are decency laws everywhere in the U.S.

1. theattemptsbycitiestobansaggypantsfallsomewherebetweendresscodesand
decencylaws

_____

_____

2. hiphopartistsmadesaggingpantspopular

_____

_____

3. plentyofpeoplearguethatthelawshouldstayawayfromfashion

_____

_____

4. thejudgesaidthatthefourteenthamendmentprotectssuchchoices

_____

_____

WORD PARTS

Directions: A **base word** is a word that can stand alone. A suffix is added to the end of a word to change how it's used in a sentence. The suffix **–ful** means *full of* (thoughtful); *characterized by* (beautiful); or *tending to be* (harmful). Write 8 words that end with the suffix **–ful** on the lines below. Share the words with the rest of the class.

1. _____   2. _____

3. _____   4. _____

5. _____   6. _____

7. _____   8. _____

Directions: A suffix is added to the end of a word to change how it's used in a sentence. The suffix **–al** turns *an action verb into a noun.* In the following sentence, see how the **verb** *remove,* which means "to take away," becomes a **noun.**

The tow truck helped in the *removal* of the wrecked car.

The suffix **–al** also can turn a **noun** into an **adjective** that describes something. For example, the noun *parent* becomes the adjective *parental.* (Sometimes the **–al** is part of the base word, so it is not a suffix, such as in the words *cereal* or *meal.*)

Write definitions for the nouns and adjectives below on the back of this sheet.

1. national	**5.** dismissal	**9.** natural
2. survival	**6.** biblical	**10.** lyrical
3. approval	**7.** tropical	**11.** spinal
4. cynical	**8.** critical	**12.** renewal

SUMMARIZING ABC's

Directions: Now that you've read the article about banning saggy pants, see how many words you can fill in the boxes below.

A–C	D–F	G–I
J–L	**M–O**	**P–R**
S–T	**U–V**	**W–Z**

SENTENCE SUMMARIES

Directions: Below are 4 key words from the article "Court Gives Saggy Pants a Lift."
Your job is to summarize, or restate, what you've learned in this article by using these
4 words or phrases in two sentences. Then, as a challenge, try to use all 4 words or
phrases in one sentence to restate the article.

FOUR KEY WORDS OR PHRASES

dress codes   U.S. Constitution
ACLU   indecent

Sentence Summaries:

1. _____

_____

2. _____

_____

Challenge Summary – (All 4 words or phrases in one sentence!)

1. _____

_____

_____

TAKE A STAND

Directions: People often have different feelings, or opinions, about the same thing. A "debate" is when people argue their different ideas. A good, persuasive argument has the following:

Facts – statements that can be proven to be true.

Statistics – research from a scientific study that uses numbers.

Examples – stories from the world that support an opinion.

You and a partner are going to debate two of your other classmates. The topic you are going to debate is the following:

> *A city should have the right to ban fashion that is offensive.*

Decide whether you agree or disagree with this statement. Then answer these questions in order to win your debate.

1. What are your 2 strongest points to persuade the other side?
(You can do Internet research to include facts, statistics, and examples.)

A. _____

B. _____

2. What will the other side say to argue against point A?

_____

_____

3. What will the other side say to argue against point B?

_____

_____

4. What will you say to prove the other side's arguments are wrong?

_____

_____

Name _____ Date _____

Comprehension: Answer the questions about the passage below.

"Many places also have dress codes. Some professions require workers to wear uniforms, and some employers limit what employees can wear. Pro basketball players follow a dress code off the court. Schools restrict what students and teachers wear. Cities are not trying to create public dress codes.

A number of places have banned saggy pants. Their laws define how low pants can be. In 2008 officials in Augusta, Georgia, considered changing its decency law. It would have made illegal 'exposure of the buttocks' but not exposure of boxer shorts. City officials finally voted not to change the law after all."

1. Why are some dress codes allowed while some fashions are banned?

_____

_____

2. What was the author's purpose for writing about this ordinance?

_____

_____

Fluency: The words in the two sentences are all connected. The sentences are also missing punctuation and capitalization. Draw slash marks (/) between the words. Then rewrite the sentence, filling in the punctuation and capitalization.

1. theaclualsomaintainsthatcommunitiescouldtargetyoungblackmenandwomenunfairly

_____

_____

2. officialsconsideredchangingpublicdecencylawsbutchangedtheirminds

_____

_____

ASSESSMENT

Fluency: Read the three sentences below. Imagine where you would pause within each sentence as you read it aloud. Draw a slash (/) mark between the phrases where you would pause. The first slash is done.

3. Now / the city will consider whether to take its case to another court.

4. In Riviera Beach most of the voters approved the ban.

5. Plenty of people argue that laws should stay away from fashion.

Vocabulary: Based on what you have learned in this lesson, match the following words with their definitions. Write the letter of the definition on the blank in front of the word it defines.

1. _____ beautiful   **A.** insulting

2. _____ offensive   **B.** finding fault with someone or something

3. _____ dismissal   **C.** what is proper for most people

4. _____ restrict   **D.** no longer allowed

5. _____ freedom   **E.** the act of telling someone to leave

6. _____ mainstream   **F.** to control or limit

7. _____ critical   **G.** the general population

8. _____ banned   **H.** liberty

9. _____ unconstitutional   **I.** pleasing to look at

10. _____ decency   **J.** violating people's legal rights